TRUANCY PREVENTION AND INTERVENTION

OXFORD WORKSHOP SERIES:

SCHOOL SOCIAL WORK ASSOCIATION OF AMERICA

Series Advisory Board

Evidence-Based Practice in School Mental Health
James C. Raines

The Domains and Demands of School Social Work Practice:
A Guide to Working Effectively with Students, Families, and Schools
Michael S. Kelly

Solution-Focused Brief Therapy in Schools:
A 360-Degree View of Research and Practice
Michael S. Kelly, Johnny S. Kim, and Cynthia Franklin

Truancy Prevention and Intervention:
A Practical Guide
Lynn Bye, Michelle E. Alvarez, Janet Haynes, and Cindy E. Sweigart

A New Model of School Discipline:
Engaging Students and Preventing Behavior Problems
David R. Dupper

TRUANCY PREVENTION AND INTERVENTION

A Practical Guide

Lynn Bye
Michelle E. Alvarez
Janet Haynes
Cindy E. Sweigart

OXFORD WORKSHOP SERIES

OXFORD
UNIVERSITY PRESS

2010

OXFORD
UNIVERSITY PRESS

Oxford University Press, Inc., publishes works that further
Oxford University's objective of excellence
in research, scholarship, and education.

Oxford   New York
Auckland   Cape Town   Dar es Salaam   Hong Kong   Karachi
Kuala Lumpur   Madrid   Melbourne   Mexico City   Nairobi
New Delhi   Shanghai   Taipei   Toronto

With offices in
Argentina   Austria   Brazil   Chile   Czech Republic   France   Greece
Guatemala   Hungary   Italy   Japan   Poland   Portugal   Singapore
South Korea   Switzerland   Thailand   Turkey   Ukraine   Vietnam

Published by Oxford University Press, Inc.
198 Madison Avenue, New York, New York 10016

www.oup.com

Library of Congress Cataloging-in-Publication Data
Truancy prevention and intervention : a practical guide / Lynn Bye . . . [et al.].
p.   cm. — (Oxford workshop series)
Includes bibliographical references and index.
ISBN 978-0-19-539849-6
1. School attendance—United States.   I. Bye, Lynn.
LB3081.T785 2010
371.2'95—dc22
2009039121

1   3   5   7   9   8   6   4   2

Printed in the United States of America
on acid-free paper

Acknowledgments

We would like to thank Paula Nauman and Phyllis Horgen for their assistance editing the manuscript. We are also grateful to R. A. M. Belland and Gale Mason-Chagil for their contribution to the case studies in this book. Phyliss Thornwaithe and Mary Ann Joseph provided valuable consultation with Chapter 7. Finally, we would like to thank Maura Roessner, Mallory Jensen, and Nicholas Liu at Oxford University Press for their encouragement, support, and assistance developing this book.

Contents

Chapter 1   Challenges Tracking and Reporting Truancy   3

Chapter 2   Federal and State Legislation on Truancy   15

Chapter 3   Truancy: Individual, School and Family Factors   29

Chapter 4   Impact of Truancy   49

Chapter 5   Best Practice in Truancy Prevention: Tier 1 School-wide
             Universal Interventions   61

Chapter 6   Best Practice in Truancy Prevention/Intervention: Tier 2
             and Tier 3   79

Chapter 7   Case Example of the Role of School Social Workers
             in a Truancy Reduction Program: South Carolina
             Truancy Pilot   95

             Appendixes 1–6   111

             References   125

             Index   137

I

Challenges Tracking and Reporting Truancy

Introduction

The first steps in truancy prevention are early identification and intervention with students who are truant (National Center for Education Statistics, 2009a). Effective systems to monitor unexcused school absences are necessary in order for interventions to be implemented before a student becomes chronically truant. To be able to evaluate the effectiveness of any truancy prevention program it is necessary to have good baseline data on the current level of the problem and an effective method of collecting ongoing data. However, there are several problems with obtaining this baseline data in schools, in states, and across the nation. This chapter will discuss the problems identifying and reporting truancy and will give recommendations for ways to solve these problems. Additionally, the role of support staff in facilitating quality attendance data collection and analysis will be discussed.

Definition of Truancy

Truancy has been identified as a serious problem in schools across the United States (Heilbrunn, 2007), and reducing it must be a priority for school social workers. Truancy is commonly defined as unexcused absence from school (U.S. Department of Education, 2008). However, what is considered unexcused, as well as the number of days students can be absent before they are required to be labeled truant, varies by state statute (U.S. Department of Education, 2008).

Consequences of Truancy

Truancy has broad, serious, and lifelong consequences and has been linked to many negative student outcomes such as lower grades, repeating grades, dropping out, substance abuse, delinquency, unintended pregnancy, gang activity, and serious criminal behavior (National Center for Mental Health Promotion and Youth Violence Prevention, 2007). One of the most important negative outcomes is the academic slippage that occurs when students miss school, fall behind, and drop out. Failing to graduate from high school places people at higher risk of earning low wages, being unemployed, having poor health, and being imprisoned (Laird, DeBell, & Chapman, 2006). Regular school attendance is "one of the most powerful predictors of whether a student will complete high school" (Heppen & Therriault, 2008, p. 1). This is particularly true in ninth grade, when students transition into high school (Allensworth & Easton, 2007).

In addition to lifelong cost for an individual, truancy also has serious financial cost for schools, communities, and society. Since state aid is based on student attendance, schools lose real dollars when students are not in school. Communities have the additional expense associated with law enforcement officers conducting truancy sweeps, and addressing the increased level of gang, drug, and criminal activities that occur when school-age youth are not in school and are not supervised. Society as a whole faces possible reductions in income tax revenue because people who drop out of school earn lower salaries and as a result pay less income tax. Society also pays the bills for the higher incidence of incarceration for this population. Heibrunn (2003) estimates that it costs taxpayers more than $200,000 over their lifetime in public expenses for each person who does not finish high school. Harlow (2003) reports that 41% of prison inmates lack a high school diploma or a GED, compared with 18% of the non-incarcerated population. In 2005–2006 it cost an average of $23,876 per year to incarcerate a person in the United States (PEW Charitable Trust, 2008).

Current Estimates of Truancy in the United States

Historically, state departments of education collected data on average daily attendance but not on truancy (National Center for School Engagement, 2006a). Starting in 2005–2006 the Uniform Management Information and Reporting System section of the No Child Left Behind Act of 2001 required school districts to report attendance and truancy rates (National Center for School Engagement, 2006a). However, Pamela Hinman, from the U.S. Department of Education, reported that although the Department of Education collects a count of truants at the district level for the Office of Safe and Drug-Free Schools, it does not aggregate the data at the state level nor publish that data due to "privacy reasons" (personal communication, June 17, 2009). Hinman further reported that state departments of education, such as the one in Minnesota, publish an attendance rate in their school report cards, rather than the truancy rate. Unfortunately, attendance rates do not accurately reflect truancy rates (Levy & Henry, 2007). Currently, each state is allowed to select its own definition of truancy, resulting in a wide range of definitions across the nation (see Chapter 2 for a summary of state definitions of truancy). The different definitions make it virtually impossible to compare truancy rates across states or regions or to determine if truancy prevention efforts are making a difference nationally (Levy & Henry, 2007).

The National Forum on Education Statistics Attendance Task Force formed the Truancy Working Group in 2006 and attempted to tackle the problem of the lack of aggregated national data on truancy. In the fall of 2007, the National Forum decided that creating a national definition for truancy was not a realistic goal because there were so many permutations regarding how long students needed to be absent from school, how often attendance was taken (each class/hour, twice a day, or once a day), how much of the day students had to be in attendance, what was considered an excused absence, and what information was obtained and recorded regarding the absence.

Following the decision to abandon the pursuit of a national definition of truancy, the Truancy Working Group reorganized as the Attendance Task Force in July of 2007 (National Center for Education Statistics, 2009a). The Attendance Task Force developed an attendance taxonomy that includes an "exhaustive, mutually exclusive set of codes" that can be used to document a student's attendance (National Center for Education Statistics, 2009a, p. 2). This taxonomy does not attempt to change state policies nor does it attempt to define truancy or excused or unexcused absence; rather, it provides a uniform method for recording absences. Although this taxonomy may be helpful in collecting and analyzing absences, we still do not have a "means of assessing the extent of truancy; definitions differ state by state, and attendance data are notoriously poor. We cannot know, as a nation, how to target resources to reduce truancy if we do not know where and among which groups of students the problem is most severe" (Smink & Heilbrunn, 2005, p. 20).

Graduation and Dropout Rates

State rates for truancy are difficult to locate because they are often not available on the websites of state departments of education, and when they are available the data frequently are not current. However, graduation and dropout rates can be used as a proxy for truancy rates because the rates are so closely linked; this is because students who are truant are more likely to drop out and not graduate from high school. Table 1.1 shows the 2005–2006 graduation and dropout rates for each state in the nation calculated by the National Center for Education Statistics (2009b). During the 2005–2006 school year the average graduation rate nationwide was 73.4 percent; individual state rates ranged from 59.8 percent in Louisiana to 87.5 percent in Wisconsin. Eighteen states had a graduation rate below the national average. The national average for the dropout rate was 3.9 percent with individual state rates ranging from a high of 8.4 percent in Louisiana to a low of 1.6 percent in New Jersey. Twenty-four states had a dropout rate at or above the national average.

Table 1.1 2005–2006 National Graduation and Dropout Rates by State

STATE	GRADUATION RATE 2005–2006	DROPOUT RATE 2005–2006
United States	73.4	3.9
Alabama	66.2	2.5
Alaska	66.5	8.0
Arizona	70.5	7.6
Arkansas	80.4	3.1
California	69.2	3.7
Colorado	75.5	7.8
Connecticut	80.9	2.0
Delaware	76.3	5.5
District of Columbia	—	—
Florida	63.6	4.1
Georgia	62.4	5.2
Hawaii	75.5	4.7
Idaho	80.5	2.7
Illinois	79.7	4.0
Indiana	73.3	2.9
Iowa	86.9	2.2
Kansas	77.6	2.4

(*continued*)

Table 1.1 (Continued)

Kentucky	77.2	3.3
Louisiana	59.5	8.4
Maine	76.3	5.4
Maryland	79.9	3.9
Massachusetts	79.5	3.4
Michigan	72.2	3.5
Minnesota	86.2	3.1
Mississippi	63.5	3.0
Missouri	81.0	4.1
Montana	81.9	3.7
Nebraska	87.0	2.8
Nevada	55.8	7.7
New Hampshire	81.1	3.2
New Jersey	84.8	1.7
New Mexico	67.3	5.5
New York	67.4	4.4
North Carolina	71.8	—
North Dakota	82.1	2.1
Ohio	79.2	4.1
Oklahoma	77.8	3.6
Oregon	73.0	4.6
Pennsylvania	—	2.8
Rhode Island	77.8	4.1
South Carolina	—	—
South Dakota	84.5	4.4
Tennessee	70.6	2.8
Texas	72.5	4.3
Utah	78.6	3.3
Vermont	82.3	—
Virginia	74.5	2.7
Washington	72.9	5.6
West Virginia	76.9	3.9
Wisconsin	87.5	2.2
Wyoming	76.1	5.7

Data from Stillwell (2009), National Center for Education Statistics report *Public School Graduates from the Common Core Data: School Year 2006–2007*

School Social Workers and Attendance Data

Why should school social workers be concerned about high-quality attendance data? Evidence-based practice is an important way to demonstrate the effectiveness of services. High-quality data is the only tool school social workers have to determine if the services they are providing or the programs they have helped to implement are really improving school attendance and reducing truancy. Also, because of their expertise in areas such as truancy, school social workers are often in a position to serve as a resource for administrators and other school personnel. School social workers can operate at the systems level and help their schools set goals to improve attendance and reduce truancy; however, to accomplish this task, a good data collection and data monitoring system is necessary. Additionally, Teasley (2004) suggests, "practitioners should research patterns of truancy in their practice domains and determine if laws and local programs are adequate" (p. 122). School social workers can also introduce programs or systems that have been effective in other schools, and collect ongoing high-quality data that will help to discern whether the program is working in their district.

Problems Identifying and Reporting Truancy

Lack of consistency is a major problem in effectively tracking school attendance data. According to the National Center for School Engagement (2005), factors that contribute to attendance data's being "wildly inconsistent" include teacher inconsistencies in reporting attendance, inflated absences, inconsistent and incorrect coding, meaningless/incorrect codes on chronic truants, and inconsistencies between school districts (pp. 1–2). For example, school staff track attendance differently even when they are in the same school and have electronic classroom tracking systems. Some teachers are simply not motivated to track and report attendance data. Attendance data may be taken in the first few minutes of a class, and students who arrive five to ten minutes late may already have been recorded as absent. Additionally, school districts generally want to portray a positive image and may have little incentive to report the rates of truancy accurately. Students who are truant may be coded as unknown or transferred or just lost in the system (National Center for School Engagement, 2005).

In addition to the inconsistency within schools and school districts, there are wide differences in the criteria for truancy among the states. This makes any meaningful comparison between the states impossible, which inhibits the ability to distinguish states that are having success in the area of truancy from those that are not. For example, the table on state definitions of habitual truancy in Chapter 2 of this book shows that in the state of Wisconsin students are considered habitually truant with five unexcused absences, whereas in the state of Connecticut students are not considered habitually truant until they have twenty unexcused absences in any month. Given the different thresholds for the number of days of unexcused absence required to be labeled habitually truant, it is clear that Connecticut would very likely have lower percentages of students reported as habitually truant.

Elements of Effective Tracking and Reporting Systems

The U.S. Government Accountability Office (2005) stresses that data must be recorded in a timely way and that the data entry system must be reliable so that regardless of the person recording the data, the information collected will always be consistent. The National Center for School Engagement (2006a) suggests that school districts answer the following questions when establishing or revising their truancy procedures:

1. What constitutes an excuse? Need it be written? If so, is an e-mail message good enough? Will a phone call suffice? Must the excuse be verified by a school official?
2. How many truancies can occur before the school is required to intervene with parents, sanction students, and make court referrals?
3. How are parents notified that their child is truant? (p. 2)

Answering these questions would help school districts to develop a clear and easily understood attendance policy, which would help with data collection as well as enforcing the policies more consistently. In addition to answering the above questions the taxonomy developed by an Attendance Task Force at the National Center for Education Statistics (2009c) allows school districts to track reasons students miss school using the following categories:

- non-instructional activity recognized by state or school
- religious observations
- illness, injury, health treatment, or examination
- family emergency or bereavement
- disciplinary action, not receiving instruction

- legal or judicial requirement
- family activity
- student employment
- transportation not available
- student is skipping school
- situation unknown (National Center for Education Statistics, 2009c, pp. 1–2)

The Absent—situation unknown category is supposed to be used temporarily only until more specific information is obtained. If states and school districts used the taxonomy developed by the Attendance Task Force, it would likely help move the nation toward a better understanding of reasons students are absent and could help school districts' staff work at a systems level to address absenteeism.

Developing a High-Quality System to Monitor Truancy

School social workers can help improve their schools' recording and monitoring systems by working with the principal to ensure that the school is using a high-quality data collection system to track attendance. School social workers need to be able to persuade others of the importance of having such a high-quality system in place, and need to be able to help implement the system or locate resources that can help implement it.

School social workers seeking to help their schools develop a high-quality system to identify and monitor truancy should work with their principal, staff, students, and parents to create: (a) a clear definition of truancy, (b) a way to consistently record and monitor attendance, (c) a method to systematically train staff in how to use the recording and monitoring procedures, (d) a clear policy regarding actions to be taken when students have missed school, and (e) a way to verify periodically that the data collected on attendance and truancy is accurate. While working on this system-wide change, school social workers can talk with administrators about conducting in-service training for teachers and office staff on the importance of early identification and intervention with attendance problems.

Helpful resources for school districts trying to upgrade their data collection and monitoring system include the National Center for Education Statistics (2005), which offers free web-based resources on "Building a Culture of Quality Data" and "Improving Educational Data." Another resource is the Truancy Reduction Application Interface Network (TRAIN), a web-based data collection and analysis program, which is available for a technical assistance fee from the National Center for School Engagement (2007). The Truancy Program Registry is also available at the National Center for School Engagement website http://www.scholengagement.org/index.cfm/ Welcome), and provides a comprehensive database of what works. Finally, the Office of Juvenile Justice and Delinquency Prevention, U.S. Department of Justice, offers a Toolkit for Creating Your Own Truancy Reduction Program, which includes helpful ideas for operationally defining truancy and establishing a data collection system and is available at the following web address: http://ojjdp.ncirs.gov/publicaions/truancy_toolkit.html.

Collecting Attendance and Truancy Data

Once a clear definition of truancy has been established and a policy has been developed that specifies steps to be taken when students are absent, school social workers need to work with their school administrators to ensure that all staff and parents in their schools are aware of the definition and related policies. School districts then need a system to train all staff about the importance of attendance, of accurately recording attendance data, and how to use the attendance codes.

When should attendance data be collected? In elementary schools where students are generally with one teacher all day attendance can be taken when school starts in the morning. In middle and high schools where students are with a different instructor each hour, attendance needs be taken at the start of each class (National Center for Education Statistics, 2009d). A consistent time needs to be established to collect attendance data in every class. Taking attendance after the first 15 minutes of class would allow teachers to greet students and get the class settled, and yet differentiate students who are absent from those who are late.

How should attendance data be collected? In the past paper was used to record attendance data in the classroom and then sent to the office to be recorded by hand by the clerical staff. However, with the increasing use of information technologies, new more efficient methods are becoming available. For example, many electronic course management systems provide a way for teachers to record several types of data including attendance in an electronic file. Schools can use data management systems that allow teachers to send their attendance data electronically to the office and eliminate the need for the office clerical staff to manually transfer the classroom attendance data into the larger school-wide attendance database.

A Microsoft Excel template can be used to track and automatically calculate several variables including attendance and is available at the National High School Center website at http://www.betterhighschools.org/pubs/ews_guide.asp. The template appears fairly easy to use and has a slot to record the student's name, the number of absences the first 20 days of school, the number of absences the first quarter of school, and the number of absences the second quarter of school. Eliminating the need for office clerical staff to manually transfer attendance data reduces another link in the communication chain where errors can occur.

In 2002 Boston Public Schools started using wireless devices to provide police officers with instant access to student information to track attendance. Previously the officers used a hardcopy printout that included information on 63,000 students in the Boston school system. The wireless device allows the police officers to identify truant students, verify their identity and notify the parents, increasing the timeliness and accuracy of the information collected (Tischelle, 2002).

Who should collect attendance data? As can be seen in the Boston example, truancy can be identified and monitored by school staff and by community members such as police officers. However, the classroom instructor is typically responsible for taking attendance and reporting the results to clerical staff in the school's office. The clerical staff is then responsible for compiling attendance records for the school. It is important to have a way to make sure that the data collection system is working and that "data submissions are mathematically correct, reasonable, consistent, and complete" (National Forum on Education Statistics, 2006, p. 15). Periodic audits where the attendance data that is sent to the office is verified can help to ensure that everyone is on the same page and that the system is working.

Conclusion

High-quality systems to monitor student attendance are essential to help reduce truancy. It is important for school social workers to take on the task of helping their schools develop and implement effective attendance monitoring systems so that they can intervene early before students fall behind academically and develop chronic attendance problems. The lack of a consistent definition for truancy in the United States prohibits an accurate nationwide assessment of this problem. Using a consistent taxonomy for truancy, such as the one devised by the National Center for Education

Statistics (2007c), would allow states to continue to determine their own individual criteria for what is considered truant, but would record more accurate data on reasons students are absent that could be aggregated at the national level.

School social workers must be concerned and involved in ensuring that their schools have high-quality data collection systems, because the consequences of truancy are so overwhelming, both personally and financially, for students, schools, school districts, and our nation. School social workers can help their school districts learn about and use elements of effective tracking and reporting systems by talking with administrators about the issue and volunteering to do in-service training with the faculty and staff on the importance of a high-quality monitoring system. This chapter described several resources that support staff can use with their schools and school districts. Our nation can do much better at identifying and intervening with students who are truant, and school social workers have an important role to play in making that happen.

◆

2

■ ■ ■

Federal and State Legislation on Truancy

Evelyn Campbell, M.S.W.,
University of Minnesota Duluth

Introduction

Truancy has been identified as a national problem (Baker, Sigmon, & Nugent, 2001). In the United States, and in countries around the world, school social workers are working to improve student attendance and address the obstacles that keep students from attending school and thus lead to truancy (Huxtable, 2007). Therefore, it is important for them to understand the complex nature of why students become truant as well as the legal process. This chapter reviews recent policies on truancy data and gives a summary of how each state defines truancy. It also illustrates the importance of school social workers' understanding policies regarding truancy and its impact on families.

Recent Policies

The No Child Left Behind Act (NCLB) was signed into law by President Bush in January of 2002. The NCLB requires that school districts submit attendance data to their state government in order to receive federal money for education (Heilbrunn, 2007). Under Title IV—Safe and Drug Free Schools Act, states are required to collect data on suspension, expulsion, and truancy (U.S. Department of Education, 2004). However, as reported in Chapter 1, states are allowed to create their own formulas for how they define truancy rates (Heilbrunn, 2007). The official website of the U.S. Department of Education states that the traditional definition of truancy is an absence from school that is not excused by the parent, legal guardian, or school administrators. State law defines how many days a student must be absent before they are considered truant (U.S. Department of Education, 2008).

State Definitions of Truancy

The National Center for School Engagement (NCSE), defines truancy as any unexcused absence from school or class without permission of the parent, teacher, or school administrator (Seeley, 2006). State law determines three criteria: (a) the age a child is required to attend school, (b) the age a child can be legally dropped from school, and (c) the number of unexcused absences to be considered legally truant. Truancy may also be considered a status offense in some states (Heilbrunn, 2006). A status offense is an activity that is illegal due to age and applies only to children. For example, smoking and drinking alcohol are legal activities for adults but not for children.

Often the definition for truancy can be found in state statutes; however, the number of days a student is absent before they are considered truant is oftentimes left up to the local school district (Zinth, 2005). Information in Table 2.1 includes a summary of definitions on truancy, habitual truancy, and penalties for all 50 states. Collecting the information in Table 2.1 was difficult and time consuming because most state department of education websites do not have an easy way to access attendance policies, especially for definitions on truancy.

Some state statutes have several sections addressing school attendance and the truancy process. For example, the Delaware attendance statute includes sections on: definitions of absence and truancy; the responsibility of police officers; notification to parents and students; absences without excuses; truancy conferences; and so on. The Maryland attendance statute includes sections on who should attend school, the ages of children who should be in attendance, exceptions to attendance and penalties, and so forth. Personal communications with state education department officials involved explanations that did not always seem practical. For example, North Carolina does not define truancy in state statute; however, it does have a compulsory attendance law, whereby failure to comply is a class-three misdemeanor. State law requires parents be warned that they may be in violation of the compulsory attendance law if their child has six unexcused absences. This state law covers truancy but it is not considered the state definition of truancy. The legal counsel for Nebraska's Department of Education wrote in an e-mail that there is not a statutory definition for "truant" or "habitually truant," therefore, they use a common definition found in the dictionary. In that case, it would be difficult for a parent to know how many unexcused absences would make a student truant.

The protocol used to obtain the information in Table 2.1 included a sequence of steps. The first step involved a review of the literature and the Education Commission of the States' website to determine if information on state definitions and penalties had been recently published. The Education Commission of the States published two documents, Zinth (2005) and Colasanti (2007), on their website which were used as a starting point when gathering information for Table 2.1. The Zinth (2005) article was the source for definitions of truancy and habitual truancy for 19 states in Table 2.1. The Colasanti (2007) article was the source for information on policies tying students' attendance and performance to driving privileges (Colasanti, 2007). The second step in the process of gathering information for Table 2.1 included examining the websites of the individual state departments of education. When information on the laws and penalties regarding truancy was not found on the website of a state's department of education, then the third step involved reviewing that state's legislative website. If information on a particular state was not located with the first three steps then the superintendent or attorney general's office was contacted.

Frequently, the state's legislative website, where laws and regulations are found, was the best place to look for definitions on truancy, habitual truancy, and penalties. These definitions were usually found under attendance codes and policies. In some states because the department of education's website was difficult to navigate and there was no clear direction about where to go to look for definitions on truancy, the state department of education superintendent's office was contacted, and in one case the state attorney general's office was contacted. Some responses came from the state department of education's legal counsel, division of data quality, attendance office, or other related offices within the department. Most states responded immediately to inquiries about their laws on truancy, although a few states did not respond.

Table 2.1 illustrates the range of criteria for unexcused absences under both the truancy definition and the habitual truancy definition for each state. For example, the second column of Table 2.1 shows that the definitions used for truancy by the states range from missing one class period in a school year to 10 or more days of unexcused absences. The number of unexcused absences increases for habitual truancy, as demonstrated in the third column of Table 2.1. Again the criteria ranged from missing one or more class periods in seven days to 20 unexcused absences in any month. In Table 2.1, the phrase "not defined in state statute" indicates that the definition of truancy and habitual truancy could not be found in state statute and may indicate that it is up to individual school districts to define it.

The last column of Table 2.1 reports the consequences in each state for truancy. Several states have school intervention programs with teams of professionals who work with families to resolve truancy problems. When students do not follow the program or plan established in the truancy intervention they can then be referred to court, where they may face driving restrictions and additional penalties. Parents may also face criminal prosecution if they do not allow for the student to attend school and do not cooperate with the school intervention program. Delaware has an extensive section on penalties in its state statute. For example, a notice is first sent to the parent that the student is absent. Then the parent and child must attend a truancy conference: afterward the school decides whether or not to file a charge against the parent. If the court determines that the parent is in violation of school attendance requirements then the parent can be fined, or imprisoned, or both. The court may also order the parents to verify the child's attendance at school, meet with school officials, take the child to school or to the bus stop, or attend school with the child, as well as undergo an evaluation in addition to other penalties. The court may also order the student to perform community service, attend counseling, undergo evaluations, and receive a reduction in driving privileges among other penalties.

These consequences for truancy are not uncommon. As the table shows, 19 states allow parents to be fined from $100 to $1000 if their child is truant. Frequently, the fine increases with the number of offenses. In Iowa, the first offense is $100, the second offense is $500, and the third offense is $1000. However, in 14 other states penalties are less explicit, parents are referred to court and may face misdemeanor charges where a fine could also imposed. For 17 states compliance with attendance policies is a condition for receiving driving privileges.

Some states' attendance policies include definitions for chronic truancy. However, in Oklahoma truancy is only defined for a child receiving public assistance, which may be withheld as a penalty for truancy. State attendance policies in New York and Montana mention the attendance of children from Indian reservations. This may illustrate their recognition of Indian tribes as sovereign nations. But it is not clear whether tribes had input into the attendance policy itself. Indian tribes may have their own solutions for

Table 2.1 Truancy Definitions and Consequences by State

STATE	TRUANCY DEFINITION	HABITUAL TRUANCY	CONSEQUENCES
Alabama	Fails to attend school without legal excuse	7 unexcused absences	Student may be placed in a juvenile facility or long-term residential care. Parent may face a misdemeanor charge and be fined, jailed or both.
Alaska	Determined by each school district	Determined by each school district	Parent may be guilty of a violation.
Arizona	Unexcused for at least 1 class period during the school year	Unexcused for at least 5 school days within the school year	Not defined in state statute
Arkansas	Determined by each school district	Determined by each school district	Student may have driving privileges suspended. School contacts prosecuting authorities.
California	Absent 3 full days in one school year or tardy or absent for more than any 30-minutes period during the school day without valid excuse on 3 occasions in one school year or any combination	Truant 3 or more times	Student may have driving privileges suspended in addition to other penalties and parents may post a bond.

(continued)

Table 2.1 (Continued)

STATE	TRUANCY DEFINITION	HABITUAL TRUANCY	CONSEQUENCES
Colorado	Not defined in state statute	4 unexcused absences in any one month or 10 during any school year	Student may be placed in a juvenile facility. Parent may be fined or jailed.
Connecticut	4 unexcused absences from school in any month or 10 in a year	20 unexcused absences from school in any month or 10 in a year	Student may be referred to juvenile court and required to pay a fine.
Delaware	3 unexcused absences from school in a year	Not defined in state statute	Student may have driving privileges revoked or suspended in addition to other penalties.
District of Columbia	Unexcused absence of a minor	10 unexcused absences	Parent may face misdemeanor charge and be fined, jailed or both.
Florida	Determined by each school district	15 absences within 90 calendar days	Student may face restricted driving privileges in addition to other penalties. Parent may face misdemeanor charge.
Georgia	5 or more days of unexcused absences	Not defined in state statute	Student may face restricted driving privileges in addition to other penalties.

State			
Hawaii	Unexcused absence by parent or school	Not defined in state statute	Student may be referred to intervention programs and/or Family Court.
Idaho	Determined by each school district	Determined by each school district	Student may face restricted driving privileges in addition to other penalties.
Illinois	Absent without valid cause for a school day or portion thereof	Absent without a valid excuse from school for 10% or more of the previous 180 regular attendance days	Student may face restricted driving privileges in addition to other penalties.
Indiana	Determined by each school district	10 or more unexcused absences	Student may face restricted driving privileges.
Iowa	Determined by each school district	No distinction between truancy and habitual truancy	Student may face restricted driving privileges in addition to other penalties. Parent who violates mediation agreement may face community service, be fined or jailed.
Kansas	3 consecutive days of unexcused absences or 5 days in a semester or 7 days in a school year	Not defined in state statute	Criminal prosecution may occur.
Kentucky	3 or more unexcused absences or tardiness	Truant 2 or more times	Student may face restricted driving privileges. Parent may face misdemeanor charge and be fined.

(continued)

Table 2.1 (Continued)

STATE	TRUANCY DEFINITION	HABITUAL TRUANCY	CONSEQUENCES
Louisiana	Unexcused leaving or checking out of school	5th unexcused absence or 5th unexcused occurrence of being tardy within any semester	Student may face restricted driving privileges in addition to other penalties. Parent may face misdemeanor charge and fined.
Maine	Half-day unexcused absence	Has completed 6th grade and 10 full days of unexcused absences or 7 consecutive school days of unexcused absences during a school year. Has not completed 6th grade and 7 full days of unexcused absences or 5 consecutive school days of unexcused absences during a school year.	Students may face several penalties. Parents may face civil violations.
Maryland	Not defined in state statute	Not defined in state statute	Students may face restricted driving privileges. Parent may face misdemeanor charge and fined, jailed, or both.

State			
Massachusetts	Determined by each school district	Determined by each school district	Parent may face misdemeanor charge and be fined.
Michigan	Determined by each school district	Determined by each school district	Parent may face misdemeanor charge.
Minnesota	Not defined in state statute, however, continuing truant is 3 or more unexcused absences if the student is in elementary school or 3 or more class periods on 3 days if the student is not in elementary school	7 or more unexcused absences if the student is in elementary school; One or more class periods on 7 days if the student is not in elementary school	Students may face several penalties and referred to county attorney.
Mississippi	5 or more unexcused absences in a school year	12 or more unexcused absences in a school year	Parent and student may be referred to court.
Missouri	10 days of unexcused absences	Not defined in state statute	None
Montana	Not defined in state statute	10 or more unexcused absences in a semester	Parent may be fined or jailed.
Nebraska	Common definition used	Common definition used	Parent may face misdemeanor charge.
Nevada	1 or more unexcused absences	3 or more unexcused absences within a school year	Student may face restricted driving privileges in addition to other penalties. Parent may be fined.
New Hampshire	Unexcused absence from school or class	20 half-days of unexcused absence during school year	Not defined in state statute

(continued)

Table 2.1 (Continued)

STATE	TRUANCY DEFINITION	HABITUAL TRUANCY	CONSEQUENCES
New Jersey	10 or more cumulative unexcused absences	Not defined in state statute	Students may face several penalties.
New Mexico	5 unexcused absences within any 20-day period	10 or more unexcused absences within a school year	Student may face restricted driving privileges in addition to other penalties. Parent may face misdemeanor charge and perform community service, or may be fined or jailed.
New York	Determined by each school district	3 or more unexcused absences	Student may be referred to court.
North Carolina	Not defined in state statute	6 unexcused absences	Parent may face misdemeanor charge.
North Dakota	1 or more hours of unexcused absence	Not defined in state statute	Penalties vary by school district.
Ohio	Unexcused absence	5 or more consecutive days of unexcused absences, 7 or more days in a school month, or 12 or more days in a school year	Student may face restricted driving privileges in addition to other penalties.
Oklahoma	Not defined in state statute	Not defined in state statute	Student may be referred to court.

Oregon	Determined by each school district	Parent may face misdemeanor charge and perform community service or be fined or jailed.
Pennsylvania	Determined by each school district	Parents receive a citation. Student may be referred to court. Parent may be fined or jailed.
Rhode Island	Not defined in state statute	Willfully and habitually absent from school	Student may face restricted driving privileges in addition to other penalties. Parent may be fined, jailed, or both.
South Carolina	3 consecutive unexcused absences or a total of 5 unexcused absences	2 or more additional unexcused absences and student fails to comply with intervention plan	Student may face restricted driving privileges in addition to other penalties. Parent may be referred to court.
South Dakota	Not defined in state statute	Parent may face misdemeanor charge.
Tennesse	Not defined in state statute	Student may have to attend truancy school. Parent may face misdemeanor charge.
Texas	Not defined in state statute	Student may be referred to court. Parent may face misdemeanor charge and be fined.

(continued)

Table 2.1 (Continued)

STATE	TRUANCY DEFINITION	HABITUAL TRUANCY	CONSEQUENCES
Utah	Unexcused absence	2 or more truancy citations within one school year	Student may be referred to court.
Vermont	Unexcused absence	Not defined in state statute	Parent may be fined.
Virginia	Determined by each school district	Determined by each school district	Student may face restricted driving privileges in addition to other penalties. Parent may be referred to court.
Washington	Not defined in state statute	Not defined in state statute	Student may be referred to court. Parent may be fined.
West Virginia	Not defined in state statute	Not defined in state statute	Parent may face misdemeanor charge.
Wisconsin	Any unexcused absence for part or all of 1 or more days from school	5 or more unexcused absences during a school semester	Student may be referred to court. Parent may face misdemeanor charge and be fined, jailed or both.
Wyoming	Determined by each school district	5 or more excused absences in any one school year	Student may be referred to court. Parent may face misdemeanor charge and be fined, jailed or both.

American Indian students who are truant. One program in northern Minnesota involves including the elders in their truancy program.

Consequences for Truancy

The number of intervention programs and consequences for truancy also vary from state to state and school district to school district. Penalties for parents range from community service to fines to imprisonment. Some state legislatures, as in Oklahoma, have been asked to enact tougher antitruancy legislation, whereby misdemeanor charges can be brought against parents whose children are truant. This may result in a parent's performing community service, being fined or imprisoned, or being both fined and imprisoned (Garry, 1996).

In seventeen states, consequences for students considered truant include having a restriction of their driving privileges (Colasanti, 2007). In Maryland, students younger than 16 years old who are considered truant may be denied a driver learner's permit (Deford, 2007). However, little research has been done on the effectiveness of this strategy.

The advantage of these penalties is that they hold the student and the parent accountable for truancy; however, the truancy laws do not take into consideration family issues. What happens when a student or parent is suffering from alcoholism or mental and/or physical health issues? What about financial issues? Families may be leery about involving a social worker for fear of losing their children to the county system or other consequences. Are these punitive approaches for truancy working? Further research needs to be done in this area to measure the success of these intervention strategies.

Role of Support Staff

School social workers need to be proactive in helping families become informed about the importance of good school attendance and the problems students face when they are absent from school, such as missed learning opportunities. School social workers also need to help parents and students learn about school attendance policies and state statutes. To fulfill their role, school social workers need to have a clear understanding of truancy laws and they need to understand what causes truancy in their school. This information will help them to determine if laws and local programs are adequate (Teasley, 2004).

Parents could be frustrated trying to find information on the state statutes for truancy because, in general, they are not easily accessible. That is why it is especially important for school social workers to keep parents informed of the current law and any changes made to it. School social workers can help implement school-wide systems to disseminate information on truancy to students and their parents. For example, school social workers could help the principal to send home flyers about the importance of good school attendance or incorporate information in a newsletter that is sent to parents about how truancy may lead to other delinquent behaviors, such as substance abuse, gang activity, and other criminal activities (Baker, Sigmond, & Nugent, 2001). With this information, families will be more informed of attendance policies and truancy laws, better prepared to deal with or prevent truancy issues, and less likely to be surprised by being found in violation of a truancy law and the severe consequence they may face. Increased awareness of the problems of missing school may encourage parents to strategize with school support staff about how to improve attendance for their child.

Family problems may be associated with school attendance, and support staff may act as a liaison, providing available resources to students and parents. Financial hardship, domestic abuse, and physical and mental health issues, as well as many other family issues, may be factors. School social workers can work with individual families to address the issues that contribute to the attendance problem. They can also help parents become more aware of the need for preventative programs such as the ones mentioned in Chapter 5, and advocate for them.

Conclusion

Overall, the definitions for truancy and habitual truancy vary from state to state and sometimes vary within each state (school district to school district). The National Cooperative Education Statistics System National Forum on Education Statistics, Truancy Working Group, decided that it is not possible at this time to have a uniform definition of truancy at the national level (National Center for Education Statistics, 2007b). Every school has an attendance policy; however, it may be unclear what is required from the student and parent. School social workers need to help the families in their schools understand the importance of good school attendance and the consequences for truancy. In some states support staff may need to advocate to their elected officials to make state laws on truancy more explicit and more accessible.

3

■ ■ ■

Truancy: Individual, School and Family Factors

Introduction

Truancy is a serious problem in the United States (U.S. Department of Education, 2009). We live in a globally competitive world and it is essential that our students be in school, on task, and gaining the knowledge and skills they will need to live in the future global economy. School social workers are particularly important in helping to remove barriers that prevent students from being successful in school, and have a long history of working to ensure that students attend school on a regular basis (Shaffer, 2007). Improving school attendance has been the focus of school social work not only in the United States, but also in many other countries around the world (Huxtable, 2007).

Truancy is a complex issue. There are multiple reasons for truancy and often more than one reason that any given student might be truant (Wesley & Duttweiler, 2005). This chapter discusses three major categories of factors associated with student truancy: individual student factors, school factors, and family factors. The chapter also highlights the interactive and cumulative effect of these factors. This chapter discusses the degree to which factors such as race, class, gender, disability (physical/learning/emotional/behavioral), sexual orientation, and intercultural parent/child conflict impact a student's educational experience so that the result is truancy and ultimately school failure.

Individual Factors and Truancy

Individual factors of disability, race, socioeconomic class (SES), and sexual orientation increase the likelihood that a student will be truant (Planty et al., 2009). Other individual student factors that contribute to poor academic performance include unmet mental health needs, alcohol and drug use, gang involvement, not viewing education as a means to achieve goals, and not feeling connected or engaged in school (National Center for School Engagement, 2009c).

Disabilities and Truancy

Truancy Case Study

By Lynn Bye and Evie Campbell

John entered kindergarten with an individual educational plan from the Early Childhood Special Education Program under speech language as a primary disability. He came to the attention of the school social worker because his attendance was sparse. The school social worker noticed John's name showing up frequently on the absentee list in the school attendance tracking system. The school social worker discovered that John's mother frequently called the school to report that her son was ill and would not be coming to school. However, when the school social worker checked with the school's nurse she was informed that other than some ear infections John did not have any major medical issues that would require him to miss so much school. John was very quiet and personable with adults but did not have much connection with other students.

Because of his high absentee rate and because the nurse's report indicated there were no serious medical conditions, the school social worker interviewed John to learn more about him and his situation. He mentioned problems at home; his mother and her boyfriend smoked and drank a lot. She also found out what kind of television programs he watched and made sure to catch a few episodes so that she would be able to talk about something that he was interested in and have a connection to his world.

John told the school social worker that he really liked art, sign language, and video games, though he was clumsy and had problems cutting with scissors. The school social worker consulted with the occupational therapist and obtained a list of activities to help him strengthen his core. Two days a week the social worker, in consultation with the physical education instructor, used these activities in an indoor recess in the gym for John and 25 to 30 other students who could benefit from structured recess play with scooter boards, jump ropes, and hula hoops. At the beginning and end of these sessions the school social worker reinforced positive behaviors.

John's mother told the school social worker that she was having a lot of difficulty getting John dressed for school in the morning and that he was refusing to go. His mother was really trying with all that she could to get him to school but she did not know what else to do because his behavior at home was volatile. She started putting him to bed dressed for school to avoid the battle she had with him every morning. At conferences she told John that he "was getting mom in trouble for not going to school."

There were times when the mother's car was not working and so the school social worker would call to make sure she had transportation to school conferences. However, his mother was very involved in conferences and other types of parent involvement and never missed a conference.

When John complained that he was having motion sickness on the bus in the morning the school social worker talked with the bus driver and asked that John be placed in the front seat and talked to the bus company to see if the route could be shortened. She found out that John was hungry in the morning because there was insufficient food that he liked in the home. The school social worker responded by going over the school breakfast and lunch menus with John, pointing out days when some of his favorite foods were served, which she thought would encourage his attendance. The mother informed the school social worker that John was on free/reduced lunch and gave permission to check to see if John qualified to have breakfast everyday. He did.

Because there were students like John who did not feel connected to the other students, the school social worker implemented a Lunch Buddy Program where about six of the students she was working with could bring a friend to her office for lunch during their lunchtime. She provided a beautifully set table with extra condiments, pickles, and healthy treats like banana bread and blueberries, which she had discovered they especially liked. Over lunch the school social worker engaged the students in topics of conversation of interest to them such as current movies, cartoons, and video games. At the end of lunch the school social worker gave them each a Hershey Kiss and Hershey Hug and escorted them back to their class for an afternoon of learning.

This school district has a policy where after three absences a letter is sent to the family stressing the importance of attendance. After five absences a second letter is sent to the family explaining consequences for truancy. After ten absences a third letter is sent saying that any further absence will result in a referral to the Truancy Intervention Program. This program brings in a lawyer who works with the school and the parents. Parents are informed about consequences of further absences. If the poor attendance continues then a letter is sent to the parents stating that the county attorney's office has been contacted about the matter and that a hearing will be held. In John's case several interventions were implemented each year to address his attendance including sending the aforementioned letter. In first and second grade two letters were sent each year and his attendance improved.

In first grade the school social worker advocated for John to be reassessed because she thought he might have fine motor problems and learning disabilities. Even with the assessment the staffing team could not determine if John was having academic problems because of his poor attendance and lack of academic exposure or if he had learning disabilities. His mother expressed concern to the school social worker that John was not learning to read. The school social worker advocated for John to be reassessed. The IEP team determined that before they would put John through another assessment for learning disabilities he had to come to school 60 days in a row. The school social worker met with John every morning when she was on breakfast duty and also saw him most every afternoon. After he missed school, when he returned she talked with him about all the fun activities he missed and how much she missed seeing him.

At the end of second grade John had missed more than 30 days. His mother was still unemployed and his parents were divorcing. The school social worker implemented an incentive system. When John made it to school three days in a row he earned a reward. The school social worker had a contract with John and his mother for attendance. She had a calendar with his name on it in her office and when he was in school on time he would come to her office and put a star on it. The star calendar was used to create a bar graph so that John and his mother could see his progress at a glance.

The school social worker also started John in a family support group where he was able to learn about family change. He was really close to his father who was moving out and the divorce was hard for him. Because of repeated attendance issues a referral to the Truancy Intervention Program was made.

Unfortunately, John's attendance continued to be a problem in third grade, and the school social worker, who had worked very hard to develop a good relationship with the mother, had to file a petition to have John's mother taken to court over the truancy issue. His mother was upset and threatened to take John out of the school and move him to another school. The school social worker was able to help the mother see that she and the other staff at school really cared about John and that transferring him would not make his problems go away. After that conversation the mother started viewing the school social worker as an advocate and ally rather than an adversary. Also, about this time the mother was diagnosed with depression, stopped drinking alcohol, and got a job.

Representatives from the court organized a meeting at school with John's parents, aunt, uncle, grandmother, and the mother's boyfriend. At that meeting a calling tree was developed so that if John was not in school the school social worker would call his father. If his father was not available, the aunt would be contacted, and so on. Release of information forms were signed so that the school social worker had permission to contact people on the calling tree. The person who was called would contact John's mother and then go get John and take him to school. They only had to use the calling tree twice.

The school social worker continued to connect with John's father on a regular basis calling him once or twice a week with updates. The school social worker was able to obtain a donated backpack and school supplies for John because he qualified as a child in need. The school social worker also made sure he was placed in a class with a caring and loving teacher. She tackled the inappropriate self-stimulating behavior by consulting health professionals and finding out that much of the behavior was due to an itch. After many conversations with John's mother and father about the self-stimulating behavior and after a special lotion was used and after John became aware that he needed to stop that behavior he was able to stop.

When John was in third grade the entire school implemented the "responsive classroom" approach. This involved morning meetings where the students had an opportunity to get to know each other better. They also did fun activities during these meetings such as sign language and games, and discussed their learning goal for the day.

It took John and his family until third grade to accomplish 60 consecutive, full days of school attendance to qualify for reassessment. When he was reassessed he was found to continue to have a speech language disability in addition to a learning disability in reading and writing. He qualified for occupational therapy services in fine motor, eye-hand coordination. The school social work services were officially added to his individual program plan to help him develop appropriate self-soothing behaviors. Additionally, his mother had him assessed by a physician and he was diagnosed with attention deficit hyperactivity disorder. However, she did not want him on any medication for that condition. The entire special education team respected the parent's request and made specific age appropriate modifications for John to be successful in the classroom. These modification included allowing him to suck or chew on something, providing him with "fidgets," which are textured rubber items that can be squeezed, and putting a "Thera-band" on the legs of his chairs which he could push against with his legs so he could be in constant motion under his desk when needed.

John is a success story. The school social worker felt that the success was due to a real team effort. During the past year he only missed two days. He has a lot of friends, is very popular; everyone likes him, and he is doing well in school. Now he is enthusiastically doing 30 minutes of reading every night and writing a response to it as part of a school-wide program. He has done this every day of the program and has also turned in his homework every day. He likes his classroom teacher, has adjusted to the divorce, is no longer in the Lunch Buddy Program, and has won an award for his attendance.

John's case study reflects the complexity of truancy cases. It also demonstrates the important role that school social workers play in reaching out to the family and the student while advocating at school for assessment and appropriate services. Often, as was the case with John, there are multiple issues that must be addressed with the individual student, the family, the education programming, and the peer group. School social workers operate from a person-in-environment perspective and are uniquely prepared to serve as liaison, coordinator, service provider, and advocate in cases of truancy. School social workers can play a significant role for special needs students and help make school a place where they want to be, therefore reducing the likelihood of truancy.

When students with disability exhibit behaviors that appear unusual or inappropriate, it is essential that those behaviors be assessed in order to efficiently determine the cause and find a solution to assist the student in addressing her/his need. Failure to accurately identify reasons for a student's behavior may result in the mislabeling of that student as having a behavioral problem, when in fact the student's behavior is in response to an unmet need. The case study provides an example where inappropriate self-stimulating behavior was observed and referred to a health care professional for an assessment. The assessment revealed that John's behavior was due largely to an itch rather than a behavioral problem. Had his inappropriate behavior not been assessed, his itch, which created the need for his behavior, would have gone unidentified with no effective solution.

Students with disabilities are often mislabeled as having behavioral problems when their learning disabilities are not accurately identified and addressed. Such labeling can begin as early as grade one. Once attached, a label such as "behavior problem" becomes extremely difficult to remove and can follow a student throughout school. This may be especially true if the student is economically disadvantaged and/or belongs to a racialized group that has been negatively stereotyped as inherently violent, tardy, and academically inferior. Each subsequent teacher reads the file of their special student in order to acquaint him or herself with the type of accommodation required to facilitate learning for that student. Thus, depending on the label and the number of suspensions a student has served, an image, usually negative, is created of the student even before the formal meeting between student and teacher takes place. The label places the student at a disadvantage because once other students become aware that a particular student carries a negative label, the labeled student becomes prey for other students, especially if the student is economically disadvantaged and is a member of an historically oppressed group.

Race and Truancy

Historically, black males have been viewed by society as the most aggressive and violent; thus this stereotype follows black youths in school and often results in a disproportionate rate of suspensions and school failure. Similarly, Hispanics and American Indians are viewed negatively by society, including the school setting, whether or not they have a disability. One high school senior reported that:

> Minority youths are often perceived as violent and a threat. As such, there is no tolerance for them, especially if they are male and economically disadvantaged. So they are not just being kicked out of schools now they are also being delivered into the hands of the police by their schools. (Haynes, 2005, p. 145)

Oakes (1985) makes the argument that the learning opportunities teachers are able or willing to create in classrooms are affected by their perception of the characteristics of the groups of students they encounter. If students come from a minority group considered less academically inclined, and if the students do not understand the instructions and feel ignored by the teacher, they often begin to disengage from school.

Labeling economically disadvantaged minority male students as having behavioral or disciplinary problems provides the schools with the justification for future suspensions and school failure. In addition, racialized parents often complain that teachers generally do not see when peers are hitting their children, but once their children, who are often the victims, respond they are then sent to the office and later get suspended for aggressive behavior. After a few years of this type of unequal and differential treatment, students begin to feel unwelcome and unwanted; thus, the disengagement process begins. During this process, students will appear disinterested in school, assignments are often not turned in, and they begin to skip classes whenever possible until they stop attending classes altogether, become truant, and eventually drop out.

It is also important to note that students often react differently to unequal and differential treatment. Students may appear either extremely angry and combative or extremely silent and broken. These two extremes may also shape the means by which students exit the educational system. For example, students who openly express objection to the unequal treatment they receive in school suffer greater suspensions and ultimately get expelled or "pushed-out" of the educational system. On the other hand, another group of students will resist in a more passive way, which often involves boycotting classes and school activities. Such students often drop out and view school and education as an oppressive system that is to be resisted at all levels. Currently, African American and Hispanic students have the highest rates of dropouts, although the rates vary from state to state (Planty et al., 2009). The challenge for many educators is to attempt to understand the nature of the resistance by marginalized students, which often manifests itself as anger and/or defiance for authority. What is required for such students who are hurting is outreach, particularly if the student is of a different racial or cultural background. As noted in the previous case study the social worker not only found out the activities John enjoyed, but she also watched the movies and gained familiarity with the games he liked to play in order to create a basis for an interactive conversation. Many Black males are required to participate in a school culture that deems them invisible except in negative terms (Hopkins, 1997). Black males are not oblivious to the pervasiveness of negative imaging and stereotyping placed on them by society at large and in turn by the public school (Hopkins, 1997; James, 1998; Nieto, 2004; McLaren, 2000; Kailin, 2004).

It is important for school social workers to be able to help students who have been marginalized to find a positive connection with a caring adult at school, because this connection helps to increase the student's sense of engagement. Allen-Meares, Washington, and Welsh (2000) noted that school social workers and other student support personnel must be acutely aware of ethnic minority "over diagnoses" with mental health disorders and overrepresentation in mental health systems (p.124). It is interesting to note that even with the high levels of over diagnosis of minority students, many of them are not being accommodated, thus are not afforded equal educational opportunity; hence the disproportionate dropout rates among certain groups of students.

No student wants to feel inferior. In an attempt to hide the internalized feelings of inferiority, they may begin to engage in disruptive behavior such as talking to a peer during class time in attempts to survive the isolation. School social workers can help reduce alienation and disassociation by acquiring knowledge of students' backgrounds and using such information to help school personnel design culturally responsive curriculums and instruction (Allen-Meares et al., 2000). They should also bear in mind that they likely do not know what a student has been subjected to and should attempt to understand the nature of the student's anger without labeling the student as aggressive, violent, or having an attitude. These labels can destroy the chance for a trusting relationship between the student and school personnel.

Sexual Orientation and Truancy

School climate has an impact on both Gay Lesbian Bisexual and Transgendered (GLBT) and non-GLBT students. Race and religion add to the complexity for gay or lesbian youth and the victimization they might endure within their families, within schools, and within their community. School social workers and teachers can enhance the educational opportunities and outcomes for GLBT youths or youths coming from a GLBT background. Currently, our educational system is somewhat tolerant toward GLBT issues, but often there often are no serious policies to safeguard and protect GLBT youths in our schools (Olson, 2008). Many of our schools have a long way to go in making our schools safe, welcoming, nurturing, and supportive to all students regardless of their sexual orientation. If students do not feel safe in their schools, they will naturally be truant and may drop out as a result.

Gay Lesbian Bisexual and Transgendered Competence Training

Many culturally competent training programs aimed at building awareness and addressing racism and other types of discrimination within our educational system and public institutions have been established throughout the

United States. Pushed by demographic changes, the society has become increasingly concerned with being politically correct or building awareness with the hope of developing greater understanding and tolerance toward each group in society. Most importantly, the call for cultural competence was meant to reduce the high dropout rates of nonwhite minority students due to racial discrimination.

We also need GLBT Competence Training for personnel at all levels in our educational system. Such training will enable educators, student support personnel, and administrators to identify students, their friends, and students from GLBT families who are at risk and to implement an early response program aimed at ensuring the success of GLBT students and their friends. It is also critical for educators at all levels to have the awareness of the signs to look for when students are targeted and to be able to engage students who may be negatively targeted. When they discover that a student is being targeted it is important that the student be provided a safe, nurturing environment, support and, if necessary, external resources. Taking these issues seriously in the schools conveys a message to GLBT students and non-GLBT students.

Much of the societal focus has been on the issues and impacts on GLBT students. What we often forget is that our non-GLBT students will also become teachers, politicians, and policy makers. We need to move toward an educational system in which our students understand that not all families have a mom and a dad, that in this country some families have only a mom, others have only a dad, and yet others have two moms or two dads. The goal is to not only widen the definition of family and make the child who is sitting on the margin move into the center like everyone else, but it is also to empower that student to speak proudly about her/his home with a single mother or father, or her/his home with two dads or two moms.

As with other marginalized groups, it is the shaming that takes place at an early stage in the educational process and which continues through the educational process that creates division and marginalization for these students and places them at higher risk for truancy. Through building awareness and becoming inclusive in our pedagogy and curriculum, we can begin to build a bridge to understanding and learning about each other as a means of building a stronger nation for all students.

Another important reason for GLBT cultural training for school educators, school social workers, and staff is to illuminate the complexities of race, religion, and homosexuality. In some communities no discussion of GLBT issues is allowed in the home. It is critical that educators have an understanding of the level of oppression a student faces when she/he comes from such a community. Students who cannot share their feelings with family or community members and who cannot share their feelings at school because of the risk to personal safety have limited options. When students see themselves as viewed negatively by peers, teachers, school staff, and society in general, alienation, disengagement, truancy and dropping out is a natural progression.

School Factors and Truancy

Two notions dominate educational policy in the United States. The first notion is that the opportunity for educational equality exists for all students, despite differences in race, culture, national identity, sexual orientation, class, and so forth. The second notion is that educational outcomes depend largely on differences in individual students' choices. The discussion in this section focuses primarily on how school factors such as stereotyping, low expectation, tracking, an inadequate multicultural approach, and a poor school climate can discourage students from attending school and lead to truancy.

We still have racist or homophobic teachers in our schools, but certainly, teachers would be less inclined to openly admit or express their racist values or homophobic views if the culture of the school did not permit it. Students continue to experience negative remarks about their ethnicity or sexual orientation. Negative comments about being GLBT can be hurtful. Students affected by these types of statements are at risk of becoming disengaged and truant.

Stereotypes and Low Expectations

Negative stereotypes related to race, class, sexual orientation, ability, and so forth can influence a teacher's perception of certain groups of students and create low teacher expectation, isolating students who are then made to feel inferior or academically deficient. In addition, negative stereotypes regarding parents' level of education, racial identity, financial resources, sexual orientation, and so forth can often impact their ability to advocate effectively and successfully for their children. The result is that their children are often truant and ultimately drop out of school. Marsiglia and Kulis (2009) note that social workers could "play an important role in working to influence policy and change the allocation of resources to improve the quality of life of members of oppressed populations" (p. 237).

Case Study: Low Expectations

By Janet Haynes

Philip's mother was desperate. Philip, her sixth grade son, arrived home from school blaming her for his difficulty in grasping the mathematical concepts he was being taught at school. His teacher told him that because his mother was a nurse's aide and his father was an auto mechanic he would not be able to grasp the complex math concept. Although the teacher knew that Phillip had a learning disability, she claimed that she was trying to alleviate the frustration the student was experiencing in learning the math concept. So, rather than investing time in helping him learn math, she determined that this student was incapable of learning certain math concepts. The greatest tragedy was that Phillip believed her and never bothered to try, despite what his mother told him. Dreams die when teachers or others in the educational system decide that they know what is good for students based on societal stereotypes. Phillip became truant and later dropped out of school.

In Phillip's scenario, his race, socioeconomic class status, and his parents' occupation, formed the basis on which the teacher developed a low expectation of his academic abilities. As a result, the teacher showed a reluctance to invest time to help Phillip acquire the skills necessary to master the math concepts he was struggling with; rather, he was encouraged to give up. Students are aware when their teachers have a lower level of expectation toward them. Phillip did not have access to a school social worker who could advocate with and for him. A school social worker could have intervened in many ways, as demonstrated in John's case example.

The United States Department of Education (2009) reports that "high academic expectations and rigor coupled with support for learning" helps students feel more connected to their school (p. 1). It is logical then that low expectations and low academic support discourage students from feeling connected.

Academic Tracking

Academic tracking is "the practice of differentiating curriculum or instruction for students based on ability levels or interest and restricting students' access to academic opportunities outside of their assigned track" (Baker, Derrer, et al., 2001, p. 416). It is essentially deciding the academic future of students by sorting them into groups of college bound, vocational school bound, or not bound for any type of higher education. Not all students in a given cohort will have the desire to become doctors, lawyers, teachers, or the future president of the United States; however, when school personnel make the choice for the student, then opportunities are automatically removed from that student. Basically, the student and his or her parent are no longer in control of his/her academic future.

Low-level tracking happens mostly to economically disadvantaged students, particularly students from racialized backgrounds, which often results in truancy and dropout. According to Orfield (2004) "It will not be surprising that the lowest performing states, many of which are located in the South, tend to serve predominantly minority and socioeconomically disadvantaged student populations. Just the opposite pattern is found among states that lead the nation" (p. 22).

Tracking of poor black and minority youths does not occur because they are unable to perform within the scope of a regular academic program, but because of racial/cultural and class discrimination within education (Nieto, 2004; Brathwaite & James, 1996). In addition, Curtis, Livingstone, and Smaller (1992) note that students are not tracked in any random way: rather, children of working-class, ethnic/racial-minority, and single-parent families end up in the lower streams in highly disproportionate numbers (Curtis et al., 1992). One mother notes "Many teachers think Black women have kids by themselves. They are always enquiring if there is a father in the home. Then they make a moral judgment and decide if the home is a good home or not" (quoted in Haynes, 2005, p. 129).

Academic tracking based on race, class, gender, marital status, and so forth, often results in disengagement, truancy, academic failure, and eventually students' dropping out or being pushed out. When a disproportionate rate of marginalized working-class youths prematurely exit the educational system, whether voluntarily or involuntarily, due to low-level academic streaming/placement, suspensions, and/or expulsions, it raises serious questions as to the process used to determine whether or not local school boards are living up to their claims of "educational equality" for all students.

Low teacher expectations are a fairly common reality for African American, Hispanic, and American Indian students, particularly those coming from poor homes headed by single mothers. However, educators, social workers, school psychologists, school counselors, and politicians often ignore this unpleasant fact of our educational system. Nonetheless, the parents, students, and community workers are all too well acquainted with this mentality that exists in our educational system. One teacher who is also a lawyer recalls the negative ways in which he was stereotyped and placed in a low level, non-academic track because of his race, class, and single status household:

> Because many of our Black single parents are working multiple jobs, it is very easy for their kids to slip through the cracks and get streamed into low-level programs without their knowledge. I was one of those kids who came from a single-parent home who got put into a low stream because they said I would not be able to study at the academic level, and because my mother was so busy working and did not understand the system, they almost succeeded. It is difficult to fight against such a system, but I am living proof that it can be done. Now, so many years later I see the same thing happening to other Black kids, but I am here to make a difference. Many of these kids are so beaten down that it's difficult to make them start believing in themselves again. (quoted in Haynes, 2005, p. 142)

The reality for many poor racialized students is that low-level academic placements disadvantage them and kill whatever dreams they may have had going through the educational system. Many minority students who are coming from single-parent households are not making it to universities. The educational system has become an oppressive place where teachers are socializing racial and ethnic minority students into the dominant, mainstream culture (Solomon, 1992). Delpit (1995) summarizes it eloquently: "Not knowing students' strengths leads to our 'teaching down' to children from communities that are culturally different from that of the teachers in the school" (p. 173). Unfortunately, many students resist the low level academic streaming or tracking by skipping school, expressing their anger, and being disciplined in the form of out-of-school suspensions, and ultimately being expelled from school or dropping out.

Educational opportunities have to be meaningful to be worth wanting and should be defined in terms of the interaction between individuals and educational institutions (Howe, 1997). School becomes less meaningful for racialized youths who are economically disadvantaged when they are placed in remedial classes not because they are unable to perform within the scope of a regular academic program, but because of racial, cultural, and class discrimination within education.

Multiculturalism and Truancy

Given the increased diversity within the United States, and despite claims of multiculturalism and equality for all students, vast educational disparity continues to exist within the educational system among marginalized groups (Planty et al., 2009). Due to the constantly changing demographics, the topic that consistently dominates ongoing debate in today's political and academic arenas with relation to equal educational opportunity and results is multiculturalism. The late Arthur Schlesinger (Martin, 2007) was one of the most prominent and vocal American critics of multiculturalism. However, others, such as the popular radio personality Rush Limbaugh, continue the argument that the *melting pot* where everyone has adopted "the" American identity is what has unified American society, and that a shared cultural identity is essential in promoting national unity.

Taking a stand against multiculturalism is no longer politically correct for educators. Thus, the arguments against multiculturalism are not readily visible in the realm of today's academic institutions. Nonetheless, the attitudes continue to be present in school policies, in the curriculum and in educational systems where a monocultural ideology continues to operate. Nieto (2000) points out that "students from dominant groups learn that they are the norm, and consequently they often assume that anyone different from them is culturally or intellectually disadvantaged. On the other hand, students from subordinated cultures may internalize the message that their cultures, families, languages, and experiences have low status, and they learn to feel inferior" (p. 64).

In a similar vein, Fleras (2001) notes that the educational system has for the most part reflected a fundamental commitment to monoculturalism and that this conformist ideology seeks to absorb immigrant children directly into society by stripping them of their languages and cultures. She argues that all aspects of schooling, from teachers and textbooks to policy and curriculum, continued to be aligned with the principles of Anglo-conformity because, "although the explicit assimilationist model that once prevailed within educational circles is no longer officially endorsed; assimilation has remained an unspoken yet powerful ethos at all schooling levels" (p. 255).

One example of the ongoing existence of the monocultural perspective in education is the way that history has been distorted to suggest that the Americas were discovered by the Europeans, which infers that Indian cultures did not exist until they were discovered by the Europeans and therefore the lands occupied by the American Indians were rightfully owned by the Europeans after they settled on and claimed them (Banks, 2004). By continuing to ignore the history between the dominant group and subjugated groups like black, American Indian, and Hispanic people, schools have reconstructed the identity of nonwhite minority students as defined by a European American perspective. This often results in the alienation of, disengagement of, and higher rates of truancy among many racialized minority students (Henry, 2007).

Understanding difference in a manner whereby it becomes a significant and valued factor in recognizing and affirming our varied history, individual identity, and collective strengths, will enable us to build an understanding of how we can use our difference to learn from each other (Dei, 1996). For example, unless we understand that differences in race are intricately tied to multiculturalism, we will not see that those who have power, or who benefit from current power relations, are not likely to be in the forefront of changing those power relations. Those who suffer most from its effects have been the primary leaders in the fight against racism. An educational system that refuses to incorporate differences in race, disability, sexual orientation, gender, class, culture, and so forth, into its policies, practice, and curriculum, and instead pretends that all students are the same, cannot also claim to provide equal educational opportunity and equal educational results. Students who are subjected daily to forms of injustices will be impacted by that differential treatment; thus, equal results become unlikely at best.

Although many educators, administrators, and public service workers have taken courses on cultural competence at some level during their career, it does not mean intolerance has disappeared. On the contrary, it may have been buried deep under educational, social, and public policies and political correctness.

Many educators, even those with the greatest intentions, have a tendency to blame students or their parents for children's educational failure without taking into consideration the student's race and socioeconomic class. It is important to reflect on how these intersecting issues impact students simultaneously and lead to truancy and eventually dropping out or being pushed out of school. There is often a tendency to examine these factors individually, which gives the impression that students face these barriers individually. The danger here is that factors such as class, race, sexual orientation, ability, and so forth, create interlocking barriers that are experienced simultaneously, rather than individually. As discussed earlier, schools continue to use the colorblind approach to schooling in order to avoid issues of racism and other interlocking factors that may impact the student's academic performance. In similar ways, despite the fact that all indicators point to severe disparity among students from certain groups, when facing issues of inequity within education, many educators experience tensions or discomfort, which often results in whites' feeling attacked or guilty and becoming defensive, silent, and/or resistant to change.

School Climate and Truancy

Can we say that the school climate provides a safe, loving, caring, and nurturing learning environment for all students regardless of race, class, sexual orientation, and so forth? How do school environments positively impact some students while negatively impacting and disadvantaging others? To what extent do educational outcomes differ because of the schools' resistance to adopt an inclusive curriculum that reflects and acknowledges the contributions of all groups and cultures equally?

Students who feel alienated or unsafe at school are less likely to attend (Reimer & Dimock, 2005). School should not be a place where some students are made to feel like they are unwelcome visitors while another group has a sense of entitlement and ownership. One such example lies in the statement of a First Nation student who said, "I think White people think education is good, but Indian people often have a different view ... they see it as something that draws students away from who they are.... I would like to tell them that education shouldn't try and make me into something I'm not" (Tierney, 1993, as cited in Howe, 1997, p. 205).

Students who do not feel connected to their school are less likely to attend and more likely to be truant (Gentle-Genitty, 2009; Belfanz, Herzog, & Mac Iver, 2007).

Family Factors and Truancy

Socioeconomic Status and Truancy

Family factors such as socioeconomic status and parent's level of education have a tremendous impact on how well students do in school. Students who do not do well in school are more likely to be truant and drop out (Baker,

Sigmon, & Nugent, 2001). In a study of 65 Los Angeles neighborhoods Lara-Cinisomo et al. (2004) found that parental educational level was the most important factor in student academic achievement. Mothers .with higher levels of education had children with higher levels of academic achievement. They also found that neighborhood poverty was an important factor in behavior problems. Students from a high poverty neighborhood were more likely to be anxious and aggressive.

Although, Lara-Cinisomo et al (2004) found that parental education and living in a poor neighborhood were the most powerful predictors of poor student achievement and student behavior, it does not mean that race is insignificant. Poverty and race often coincide. According to the report, The Condition of Education 2009, published by the National Center for Education Statistics (2009e), 'A greater percentage of Black, Hispanic, and American Indian/Alaska Native students attended high-poverty schools than did White or Asian/Pacific Islander students in 2006–07.... High poverty schools are defined as public schools where more than 75% of the students are eligible for free or reduced-price lunch' (NCES, 2009d, p. 64). The question here is: If education is getting better for these groups of students, then how do we explain the statistics in Table 3.1 that show that American black and Indian students have the lowest graduation rate in most regions of the United States? It is important to note that three groups—black, Hispanic, and American Indian/Alaska Native students—attend the nation's poorest schools, and students from these ethnic groups also have the lowest graduation rates (see Table 3.1).

Table 3.1 2004–2005 National and Regional CPI Graduation Rates, by Race and Ethnicity

NATION

All Students	68.0
American Indian/AK Nat	67.2
Asian/Pacific Islander	90.5
Hispanic	64.2
Black	60.3
White	80.4

Source: National Center for Education Statistics. (2009). Common Core of Data.

In addition to poverty, other family factors associated with truancy include a lack of parent supervision and/or guidance and a lack of awareness of school attendance laws (U.S. Department of Education, 2009). The majority of parents work full-time outside of the home and many hold down two jobs and still have trouble paying their bills. Mental illness and or chemical dependency may also make it difficult for parents to provide their children with the supervision necessary to make sure that their homework is completed, that they are adequately fed, and that they are prepared to be successful in school (Henry, 2007).

Conclusion

A myriad of interacting individual, school, and family factors play a significant role in whether or not students are truant, drop out, or are pushed out. Individual factors of disability, race, socioeconomic class, and sexual orientation increase the likelihood that a student will be truant. School factors that perpetuate structural inequality and lead to truancy include stereotyping students, holding low-expectations for students, tracking students in remedial programs based on stereotypes, and poor multicultural understanding among school personnel. Family factors associated with truancy include poverty, educational level of parent, chemical dependency, and emotional problems.

Teachers, social workers, and other school personnel do not have to identify as black, Hispanic, American Indian, GLBT, or as a person with a disability to express support and share the pain inflicted as the result of homophobia, racism, or classism that GLBT, minority, and economically disadvantaged students suffer. Love, understanding, and support can make the difference in whether a student attends school or feels that she or he does not belong and becomes truant. School social workers have a special role to play in addressing the complex individual, school and family factors associated with truancy. Creating a school environment for *all* students that is positive, safe, respectful, supportive, academically challenging, and honoring of their differences is important in the effort to reduce truancy.

4

■ ■ ■

Impact of Truancy

Introduction

Truancy negatively impacts students in several ways. Students who are truant
are more likely to fall behind academically, drop out of school, use drugs and
alcohol, and be involved with the criminal justice system (Smink &
Heilbrunn, 2005). This chapter begins by examining school discipline in
relation to truancy and school dropout. It is important to understand that
unequal application of school discipline can impact a student's decision to
stay or to leave school. In discussing school discipline, this chapter looks at
the unequal application of discipline in schools and existing racial disparities
in school discipline. In addition, the chapter explores the ways truancy
impacts the individual students, the school system, and society. All three of
these levels pay a high price for truancy.

School Discipline and Sense of Connectedness

When students become aware that they are in an educational system that does
not value their presence, fading or disengaging is the natural next step for the
student (Pellerin, 2000). The student may think, "What does it matter if I
don't show up for class?" or, "Who is going to miss me?" Students may begin to
believe they are invisible. For example, the author of this chapter had
students ask, "Why should I be in a class where the teacher does not want
me there?" When students feel they are not wanted they often have difficulty
focusing on the reason they are in school in the first place: their academics
(National Center for School Engagement, 2009a). Rather, the student's primary concern becomes focused on surviving an educational system that is un-
nurturing, hostile, unwelcoming, and that marginalizes them. With that
mindset, students can begin to react in a self-destructive manner due to the

hurt and shame. Unequal and exclusionary educational policies and practices alienate students.

Students often become disengaged when schools do not provide a structure whereby they can safely and effectively address the issues that impact their daily school experiences in a manner that validates their emotion. Without such a structure the feelings of rejection, alienation, and isolation are left to fester. The sense of unequal treatment and opportunities often results in students becoming angrier, more reactive, disengaged and/or silenced. According to Hardy and Laszloffy (2007), "Suppressed anger is the seed of rage. Over time anger grows and intensifies until eventually it is transformed into rage, a far more intense, sustained and consuming emotion" (p. 96). The strategy that students usually adopt when they are resisting an unfriendly school environment is one of truancy, disengaging, and ultimately dropping out or being pushed out via expulsion (Osterman, 2000). But, in the student's mind, it may be a form of resistance against a system that devalues his or her presence.

School personnel often interpret these reactions as inappropriate, aggressive, and a threat to the social order. This is particularly true when students fit a stereotype. Given that African American male students are often stereotyped as being aggressive and violent, it is not surprising that they have the highest rates of suspensions and expulsions (Planty et al., 2009). Table 4.1 shows suspension rates by ethnic groups for 2006. It is clear from Table 4.1 that the percent of African American students suspended from school is almost double that of any other ethnic group.

Table 4.2 shows the percent of students expelled from school in 2006 by ethnic group. Again, African American students have the highest percent of expulsions.

Table 4.1 Suspensions in 2006

AFRICAN AMERICAN STUDENTS	AMERICAN INDIAN/ ALASKAN NATIVE	HISPANIC	WHITES	ASIAN/ PACIFIC ISLANDER
15%	8%	7%	5%	3%

Table 4.2 Expulsions in 2006

AFRICAN AMERICAN STUDENTS	AMERICAN INDIAN/ ALASKAN NATIVE	HISPANIC	WHITES	ASIAN/ PACIFIC ISLANDER
5%	3%	2%	1%	1%

When students are not in school because they are out on suspension or expulsion, the educational gaps become even wider because they are missing instruction (Hubbard, 2005). It is logical that the more frequently a student is suspended the wider the educational gap will become and the greater the chances will be of the student's dropping out. The reality is that suspensions frequently result in poor academic outcomes, which lead to an increased likelihood of dropping out. More importantly, the message being sent to the individual student is that he or she is neither valued nor wanted. This is particularly true when they see peers of a different race or ethnic group suffering less severe consequences for similar behaviors. The National Center for School Engagement, "advocates never suspending or expelling a child for truancy" (Heilbrun, 2007, p. 9).

School personnel reaching out to students in an engaging manner that develops a trusting, respectful, relationship is an important first step in reducing truancy. Students, regardless of race, class, gender, or ethnicity, need a nurturing and welcoming learning environment. They need to know that school personnel care about what is important to them and the factors that negatively impact their learning. Teachers need to take time to attempt to understand the student and acquire some knowledge about the student's cultural background because "knowledge of culture is one tool that educators may make use of when devising solutions for a school's difficulty in educating diverse children" (Delpit, 1995, p. 167). This is especially true when students are from a different race or ethnicity than the teachers. Such a relationship is essential not only to develop an understanding of the student's mannerisms and responses, but also to develop a trusting relationship between student and teacher. Establishing a strong, positive relationship can be particularly challenging for the teachers from the dominant culture who are teaching in high poverty schools where students are dealing with various barriers.

Once a trusting relationship is established between the teacher and student, the teacher will be able to recognize more readily the student's academic potential rather than making assumptions based on stereotypes. In return, the relationship will reinforce the student's academic worth and will help the student develop a positive attitude toward school and his or her potential, thus increasing the chance of an equal outcome. Affirming the student's academic worth motivates the student to excel academically, thus achieving his or her full academic potential.

Impact of Truancy on the Individual Student

Educational Gap, Unequal Outcomes, and Dropping Out

The educational gap and the high rate of dropout have consistently been of concern to educators, parents, and policy makers. Research has shown that African Americans, American Indians/Alaskan Natives, and Hispanics have the highest dropout rates; these three groups are also made up of the students attending high poverty schools (National Center for Education Statistics, 2009b). High poverty schools have fewer resources compared to schools that are not high poverty.

Research has also shown that the high poverty schools tend to attract teachers who are less experienced and qualified compared to high-income schools (David, 2008). The National Governor's Association (2004) reported that, "among low-income schools, nearly 20 percent of teachers leave every year. On the other hand, less than 13 percent of teachers in high-income schools leave each year. In addition, low-income schools are much more likely to have teachers teaching subjects, especially math and science, in which they do not have a major or minor, as compared to more 'desirable' schools" (p. 42). Due to the quality of teacher preparedness and motivation, the achievement levels of high-income schools are significantly higher. This is supported by statistics that show that a higher percentage of whites and Asian/Pacific Islanders attended high-income schools. Statistics also show that Asian/Pacific Islander students are among the highest achievers. So, naturally, the dropout rates will be higher and the educational gaps will be wider for American Indians, Hispanics, and African Americans. Despite the arguments around equal educational opportunities and the belief that all students are offered equal opportunity within our educational system, the fact that these three groups attend the nation's poorest schools suggests that they do not have the same opportunity for educational success as their white and Asian counterparts who are attending high-income schools (Alberts, 2009). It is also important to note that the educational gap, the academic outcome, and the dropout rates are significantly higher for males than for females for all groups (National Center for Education Statistics, 2009b).

Truancy is associated with poor educational outcomes. Students must be attending school to be able to learn because when they are absent from school, they miss instruction on academic topics (Chang & Romero, 2008). It requires extra effort on the student's part to obtain the information they missed because they need to find some way to obtain the information, such as asking a peer for notes (and that assumes that the notes are accurate and will be helpful) or making an appointment with the teacher to find out what was missed and how that information can be obtained. This can be more than challenging for students in high poverty schools who are struggling to cope with personal, family, community, and/or social issues. If the student does not feel engaged or connected with the school or teacher, there is less likelihood that the student will take the initiative to approach the teacher because of a sense of vulnerability.

Educational gaps occur when students are absent from school. This is particularly true in classes where the knowledge and skills build sequentially on previous information; any missed classes can create a real problem for learning new content when part of the foundational knowledge is missing. School becomes very difficult when students fall behind. Once students fall behind academically, it may seem overwhelming for them to catch up and much easier for them to give up and drop out of school. There can be a snowball effect, particularly with no intervention or support.

The intersecting prejudices a student faces, such those that involve race, class, sexual orientation, family difficulties, learning disabilities, and so forth, are cumulative. When barriers far outweigh the resources or support available to the student, the risk of internalization increases, thus decreasing the student's chance for educational success. It is less likely that the student will remain in school. Consider a learning disabled student who is economically disadvantaged, struggling with sexual identity, and coming from a homophobic home and community. Given the student's sexual orientation, it is also likely that the student may be subjected to peer bullying both at school and within the community. If this student internalizes the intersection of the various "isms" he/she becomes at increased risk of suicide. According to Hardy and Laszloffy (2007), expressing emotions that expose one's vulnerability can be costly within youth culture. Whom can he talk to? Where can he turn?

Another example that could yield a different form of self-destructive behavior would be a racialized, economically disadvantaged student in the same high poverty school, living in a high crime area, who is experiencing difficulty in school. Without intervention, that student also becomes at risk of truancy and ultimately dropping out. As mentioned, if this student believes that it is necessary to be tough, then this student becomes at risk of becoming a bully as a defense mechanism to hide the hurt and pain (Hardy & Lazloffy, 2007). Students that drop out often face a sense of personal failure, disappointed parents, and a great sense of loss toward future goals. Once the student drops out of school, without encouragement and support, it is this sense of loss that causes the student to become hopeless and at risk of turning to the wrong peer support group to find comfort, acceptance, a sense of belonging and a positive sense of self.

It is important for student support personnel to be able to identify, in both scenarios, youths who are experiencing multiple interlocking barriers. It is equally important to identify at a very early stage students who may be internalizing or students who are masking their pain. For example, when a low/underachieving student tells a school social worker, "I don't care that I failed the math test," but is not able to maintain eye contact with the social worker, the behavior should not be misinterpreted. School personnel should not assume that the student does not want to be in school, or get good grades, or has bad work habits, or lacks discipline, or is unable to meet the academic challenge. Behavior must always be understood in context. The student may come from a culture where eye contact is not appropriate when speaking with an adult. When working cross-culturally, caution must be taken when interpreting student's nonverbal messages in order to ensure that the lens is not assigning new meaning to the student's behavior.

It is essential that social workers in cross-cultural, cross-racial relationships not take a student's comment at face value. The student's educational history must also be taken into consideration. For example, if the student was subjected to low teacher expectation, it is possible that the student suspects the social worker may have the same low expectations. The social worker's ability to effectively engage the student in a discussion can potentially alter the educational path of that student in a positive way.

Truancy and Alcohol, Drugs, Gangs, and Crime

High rates of alcohol and drug use are associated with truancy (Duarte & Escario, 2006). Youths who are truant from school and live in neighborhoods that have a high concentration of drug and gang activity become at risk of becoming involved in those activities. Students who are not in school and are not at home can be reasonably assumed to be in the community associating with peers who are not in school or with adults and may already be involved in criminal activity.

As previously discussed, youths who are beginning to act tough to mask the hurt or alienation they are feeling from school will also need to display this level of toughness in their community. The problem here is that youth who have not been involved with gangs or who have not been associated with individuals involved in criminal behavior become at risk of being intimidated and coerced. Students who are truant are also much more likely to be involved in gangs and in trouble with the law. Walker, Spohn, and Delone (2007) argue that in neighborhoods where gangs are prevalent, young people often experience tremendous pressure to join a gang simply as a means of personal protection. They further argue that "because of residential segregation based on income and race, a person who is poor, a racial or ethnic minority, or both is more likely to have personal contact with people who are already involved in crime" (p. 93). Therefore, students who are truant from school or who drop out of school return to the neighborhood in which they live.

If Sutherland's theory holds true, then naturally these students will come into contact with gang members and may be recruited, if not because they are seeking protection, then as a means of establishing an income. Research has shown that because a higher percentage of males drop out and become truant, they are at greater risk of becoming involved in drug and gang activity and ultimately becoming incarcerated or killed than are females (National Center for Education Statistics, 2009f).

Truancy is a statutory offence, and when students are truant it can put them into the criminal justice system. Given that African Americans, American Indians, and Hispanics make up the largest group of dropouts, and given that they also tend to live in high poverty areas, it is not surprising that students from these three groups are at greater risk than their white or Asian counterparts. This data "suggests a grim future for a large percentage of racial and ethnic minority children" (Walker et al., 2007, p. 82). Therefore, it is reasonable to expect that the incarceration rate for African Americans,

American Indians, and Hispanics will be greater than for Asians or Whites. The research has established that there is a high correlation between race, poverty, truancy/dropout rates, and crime (National Center for Education Statistics, 2009f; Reyhner, 1992; Orfield, 2004).

Basically, in addressing issues of truancy, gang activity, and crime the issue of poverty cannot be ignored. According to Maslow's (1987) hierarchy of needs, basic human essential needs of housing, food, and clothing must be met. This need does not change for students who have dropped out or who were pushed out of the system due to suspension or expulsion. How do they exist with a marginal education living in a high poverty, high crime area within an economically disadvantaged household? A mother's dream is for her child to break the cycle of poverty through education. Thus, when a young student drops out of the educational system the chances of achieving upward mobility are slim. Options are reduced and criminal involvement, in the form of drugs or other criminal behavior, becomes more appealing as a means of economic survival.

When ethnic minority students, particularly males, living in a high crime area become inducted into the criminal justice system the chances of gainful employment are further decreased due to a lack of a high school diploma coupled with a criminal record (National Center for School Engagement, 2009e). It is important to note that students graduating from high-income schools do not have to explore these avenues for their economic survival. Theirs will be a natural progression into college if they so choose.

Impact of Truancy on the School System

School districts lose revenue, risk having overall lower test scores, and can develop a poor reputation when students are truant. Students who are truant are being undereducated and less prepared for a life of productive citizenship. With the No Child Left Behind Law, school districts are expected to help their students make "adequate yearly progress" and when they do not make adequate progress, schools risk being sanctioned (Heilbrunn, 2007). In low-income schools where 75% of the students are on free and reduced lunch, the majority are African American, American Indian, and Hispanics. These ethnic groups also represent the highest groups of students dropping out in the nation. Schools with low academic scores and high dropout rates face greater financial problems because they are losing funding due to students' poor academic performance. In addition, students in low-income schools who may require specialized services beyond the classroom are further left behind due to lack of funding. For instance, a student requiring reading assistance my not receive it, even though it is required by his/her educational plan (IEP), due to the fact that the district may have inadequate income to meet the staffing needs. Nonetheless, despite funding cuts, high poverty schools are expected to pay for increasing operating costs, which reduces the ability to recruit teaching staff at competitive rates.

Additionally, with reduced funding schools must operate with outdated equipment, libraries and computers cannot be updated, teaching supplies are reduced, and teaching/learning resources and supplies for students are either marginal or no longer available. Marginalized students lose out on valuable field trips to places such as science museums and historical sites due to the fact that funding for their school was cut. Therefore, students are further disadvantaged because of financial crises. High poverty schools must consistently find ways of reducing operating budgets based on new funding criteria. Thus, when compared with high-income schools, where students are performing well academically, low-income schools must find alternate means of meeting the rising costs of teaching and student supplies (National Center for School Engagement, 2006b).

Impact of Truancy on Society

Truancy has many negative outcomes for society, such as a less educated workforce, higher crime rates, and increased costs for the criminal justice system (James, 2004). When students are truant from school and drop out, the result is a less educated workforce (Smink & Heilbrunn, 2005). This results in the undereducation of students from certain racialized groups that, in turn, create generational poverty because families are not able to break the cycle. The continued generational cycle of poverty contributes to and normalizes welfare dependency and living in a community ridden with criminal activity. Crime is a reality for many families who have generational cycles of incarceration. It is plausible to have a grandfather, a father, and a son murdered due to criminal activity. This tragedy stems from the need for survival and the need to support one's family members. The reality is that a young male becomes an adult, takes a wife and has children, and then has to find ways to support that family. Not having a high school diploma makes it difficult to support the family. However, having a criminal record makes it virtually impossible to access gainful employment.

High crime rates are indicative of high poverty and unemployment rates in communities. They also result in high levels of violence and also poor quality housing and rundown or burned out properties. Walker et al. (2007) observe that:

> Crime has a devastating impact on neighborhoods. . . . First, it results in direct economic loss and physical harm to crime victims. Second, the resulting high fear of crime damages the high quality of life for everyone in the area. Third, persistent high rates of crime cause employed and law-abiding people to move out of the neighborhood, thereby intensifying the concentration of the unemployed and high-rate offenders. (p. 91)

Conclusion

This chapter reviewed the impact of truancy on the individual student, on the school system, and on society. In examining the impact on individual students, school discipline and climate along with poor academic outcomes and dropping out were discussed in relation to the possible ways they can impact the individual student. Important to the discussion was the highlighting of racial disparities in the application of school discipline. The chapter also looked at ethnicity in relation to truancy, educational gaps, and poor academic outcomes and rates of dropping out of school. Critical to the discussion was the correlation between the dropout rate for African Americans, American Indians, and Hispanics in relation to drugs, alcohol, gangs, and crime.

In relation to the impact of truancy on the school system we examined the ways in which poor academic performances results in lost revenue for high poverty schools. Discussions also centered on the impact on high poverty schools in terms of operating costs, recruiting teachers, and maintaining up-to-date equipment and resources for students and teachers. In reviewing the research, it is clear that when high poverty schools face funding cuts this has a direct impact on students who are already economically disadvantaged. In other words, when compared to high-income schools, the research shows that students attending high poverty schools face an uphill battle in achieving equal academic outcomes.

The impact of truancy on society is equally troubling. Communities with high rates of truancy experience higher rates of crime and gang activity. Ultimately, society ends up paying the cost of the lost potential of many of its citizens as well as paying the cost of criminal prosecution and incarceration. As a society we need to look at the cost effectiveness of the current policies and find better ways to keep students engaged in school. Several resources are available to help with this effort such as the "Tool Kit for Creating Your Own Truancy Reduction Program" (U.S. Department of Justice Office of Juvenile Justice and Delinquency Prevention, 2007) and the "Fifteen Effective Strategies for Improving Student Attendance and Truancy Prevention" (Smink & Reimer, 2005). School social workers can play an important role by helping their schools take the initiative to explore and implement evidence-based approaches to improving school attendance and reducing truancy.

5

■ ■ ■

Best Practice in Truancy Prevention: Tier 1 School-wide Universal Interventions

Introduction

This chapter reviews resources for identifying research-based programs that address truancy prevention, criteria to consider when selecting a program, readiness for program implementation, and offers a case study that examines the program implementation process. The chapter describes the Response to Intervention (RtI) system, which addresses student needs by monitoring student progress, that is, following an intervention to ensure positive student outcomes (Batsche et al., 2005). Tilly and Clark (in press) define RtI as, "a multi-tiered framework for organizing evidence-based practices in a systematic process for the purpose of determining what interventions ensure the academic, social, emotional, and behavioral success of all students" (manuscript p. 5).

Strategies utilized to address an issue in Tier 1 reach 80%–90% of students and are termed universal or schoolwide because they are delivered to all students in school (NASP, 2002). In this approach student performance data are continuously used to match high quality instruction and supports to the needs of all students. Information is provided in Chapters 5 and 6 on both prevention and intervention strategies; however, the emphasis should be placed on early school-based intervention as opposed to addressing chronic truancy (Capps, 2003; Mogulescu & Segal, 2002; Mueller, Giacomazzi, & Stoddard, 2006). McCray (2006) notes that the current literature focuses on the need for schools to address attendance problems early to prevent students from dropping out; however, the definition of "early" has changed from a high school or middle school focus to kindergarten. Research-based interventions for risk factors, such as truancy, that impact student success begin as early as pre-K (SAMHSA, 2009). The emphasis in the next two chapters is on the comprehensive continuum of services that needs to be provided to students and families, and the early intervention that is present in a Tier 1 RtI approach to addressing truancy.

Identifying Best Practices

With the continued emphasis placed on accountability and the recurring focus on the use of research-based programs to address the needs of students, accessibility to information on interventions and strategies that are empirically supported is available on the Internet. Websites such as those developed by the United States Department of Health and Human Services Substance Abuse & Mental Health Administration (SAMHSA); the United States Department of Justice Office of Juvenile Justice and Delinquency Prevention (OJJDP); the Center for the Study and Prevention of Violence, Institute of Behavioral Science at the University of Colorado at Boulder; and the What Works Clearinghouse (WWC), United States Department of Education, Institute of Education Sciences provide practitioners with sophisticated reviews of research-based programs that address issues faced by students. The URLs for these websites are provided in Table 5.1.

Each site provides a description of the level of research base that must be utilized in the review process of programs listed on their sites. The National Registry of Evidenced-based Programs and Practices (NREPP) developed by SAMHSA notes that,

> In the health care field, evidence-based practice (or practices), also called EBP or EBPs, generally refers to approaches to prevention or treatment that are validated by some form of documented scientific evidence. What counts as "evidence" varies. Evidence often is defined as findings established through scientific research, such as controlled clinical studies, but other methods of establishing evidence are considered valid as well. Evidence-based practice stands in contrast to approaches that are based on tradition, convention, belief, or anecdotal evidence. (2009)

This serves as a reminder to practitioners that it is no longer acceptable to select an intervention without knowing that it has proven successful with the target population. In addition to providing a definition of the evidence

Table 5.1 Evidence-based Intervention Websites

ORGANIZATION	WEB ADDRESS
Center for the Study and Prevention of Violence Institute of Behavioral Science at the University of Colorado at Boulder	http://www.colorado.edu/cspv/blueprints/index.html
National Dropout Prevention Center/Network	http://www.dropoutprevention.org/effstrat/default.htm
United States Department of Education, Institute for Education Sciences (IES)	http://ies.ed.gov/ncee/wwc/reports/topic.aspx?tid=06
United States Department of Justice Office of Juvenile Justice and Delinquency Prevention (OJJDP)	http://ojjdp.ncjrs.gov/programs/ProgSummary.asp?pi=36
United States Department of Health and Human Services Substance Abuse & Mental Health Administration (SAMHSA)	http://www.nrepp.samhsa.gov/
Sample State Resource Page	http://www.pde.state.pa.us/svcs_students/cwp/view.asp?a=141&q=96008

base on each of these sample websites, the criteria for assessing the quality of research is provided at the website and includes "reliability of measures, validity of measures, intervention fidelity, missing data and attrition, potential confounding attrition, [and] appropriateness of analysis" (SAMHSA, 2009). The OJJDP model programs are evaluated utilizing similar criteria and programs are classified into the categories of *exemplary, effective,* or *promising* (OJJDP, 2009). Finally, the National Dropout Prevention Center (NDPC) also provides a database of programs reviewed for level of effectiveness supported by research. These websites provide a point to begin research on evidence-based programs that address truancy in a school setting. The very descriptive nature of sites such as NREPP allows the practitioner to make initial decisions about the fit of the program with the school.

Considering Goodness-of-Fit in Selecting Programs

For the most part, the websites noted above provide the practitioner with information about the program purpose, targeted outcomes, appropriate age for intervention, populations studied in reporting participant outcomes (age, gender, race), settings studied (urban, rural) and costs of training and curriculum (SAMHSA, 2009). When selecting a program that could successfully be implemented in a specific school district, it is important to look closely at this descriptive information. For example, if the school district is located in a rural area, has the program research included studying outcomes for students in rural districts, is the diversity of the population of that school addressed in the research?

When assessing costs, pay close attention not only to the price of the curriculum materials but also to the format of training provided. How much training is required to implement the program? Who must be trained? Where is the training located, and how much are travel and registration costs? Is on-site training available, and does this cost less than sending a few staff members to be trained (other school districts might be interested in the training and willing to share costs)? Is there a train-the-trainer model that enables a school district to send several staff members to be trained and then have them come back to the district and train others (this increases the chances of sustaining a program if the person trained leaves their position with the district)? The U.S. Department of Education provides very detailed information on selecting a research-based program at www.ed.gov/admins/lead/safety/training/selecting/index.html.

When preparing to implement a research-based program, there are several steps that must be taken to ensure successful implementation and continuation of the program. First is creating a readiness for change. As different programs are being considered, support staff can solicit input from key stakeholders in the implementation process. If the program will be implemented in the classroom, identify teachers to assist in program selection. If the program will be implemented in all building locations, include staff from the cafeteria, library, environmental maintenance, bus drivers, front office, teachers, and classroom aides in the selection process.

Creating a diverse group to select the program will provide additional support for the program's implementation. Next, present the program to all school-building staff. Answer questions about the program and provide them with descriptions of potential student outcomes as a rationale for offering the program to students. Explain the role of different school staff in the program.

Slavin (2004) notes that, "The whole school must make a free and informed choice to adopt SFA [the program/curriculum]; we require a vote by secret ballot of at least 80%" (p. 62). The developers of other research-based programs such as Positive Behavioral Interventions & Supports suggest this same 80% level of "buy-in" by school personnel.

Once the program has been selected and there is support for its implementation, an infrastructure for implementation must be developed. Every staff member should know his or her roles and responsibilities in implementing the program. Training for a research-based program will include a manual for program implementation, the curriculum, evaluation instruments, and an instrument to measure the fidelity of implementation. Fidelity of implementation measurement refers to the process of implementing a program, and questions whether the practitioner/school personnel follow the steps outlined in the curriculum manual exactly as they are written by the program developer. Implementing a program exactly as prescribed in research studies is more likely to produce similar outcomes. However, in some cases adaptations of the prescribed program must be considered. Table 5.2 provides sample lists of implementation checklists.

Table 5.2 Implementation Checklists

PROGRAM	SAMPLE IMPLEMENTATION CHECKLIST
Positive Behavioral Supports & Interventions	www.pbis.org/common/pbisresources/tools/ebsteamchecklist.doc
Olweus Bullying Prevention Program	www.fasa.net/upload_documents/SchoolwideFidelity**Checklist**.pdf
Multiple Program Implementation Checklist	*captus.samhsa.gov/northeast/PDF/evalmodelprog_vt.pdf*
Attendance Outreach	www.highschooltoolkit.com/ToolKitTopics/Attendance%20**Checklist**.pdf
Second Step and Steps to Respect	http://www.cfchildren.org/support/success/

With the emphasis placed on implementing a research-based program exactly as it was studied, practitioners need to be aware of adaptations that the program developer has found successful in schools implementing the program. Often the developer has had contact with the schools and assisted them in considering the impact of adaptations made to the program. Raines (in press) suggests that practitioners always consider three types of program adaptations:

1. Developmental adaptations (age group and social/cognitive skills of the targeted population)
2. Cultural adaptations (when appropriate does the program take into account protective factors and stressors specific to a minority group or family, and recognize differing levels of acculturation in the culture within a family, and are there culture specific traditions that can be incorporated into the curriculum?)
3. Contextual adaptations (format for implementing the program in a school setting, e.g., time of day, length of time)

Another important step in program implementation is program evaluation. DeSocio et al. (2007) identify the inclusion of a formal program evaluation by an independent evaluator to be a best practice in implementation of interventions to address truancy. Partnering with a local university professor is one method of combining the need for an independent evaluator with the requirement of university faculty to conduct research. Often universities have money available for faculty to conduct research; these funds can help offset the costs of contracting for evaluation services. Raines and Alvarez (2006) provide an example of such collaboration:

> A local school district and community mental health agency applied for an elementary and secondary school counseling program grant to prevent school dropouts. After meeting once as a group and agreeing on the basic concept, they divided up the roles. A university researcher was assigned the initial needs assessment to establish baseline data, the community agency people investigated evidence-based programs to reduce school dropouts, the school personnel worked to adapt these approaches to their rural district, the community agency identified which resources they could supply to make the program work, and the university professor planned the program-end evaluation. (p. 47)

To sustain a program that a school district has implemented, it is then important to publish the results (outcomes) in both academic journals and local sources, such as newspapers, magazines, and school district promotional materials.

Funding for Large and Small School Districts

Funding for programs that address attendance (prevention) and truancy (intervention) is available at the local (e.g., business and family foundations that fund

Table 5.3 Funding Truancy Prevention in a Town in Minnesota

LEVEL OF FUNDING	FUNDING SOURCE
Local Community	Educare Foundation (http://www.educarefoundation.org/news.php)
	Mankato Area Foundation (http://mankatoarea foundation.com/)
	City of Mankato (http://mankato-mn.gov/Community-Grant-Program/Page.aspx)
	Best Buy Foundation (http://communications.bestbuy.com/communityrelations/our_foundation.asp)
	WalMart Foundation (http://walmartstores.com/CommunityGiving/203.aspx)
State	Minnesota State Bar Association (http://www2.mnbar.org/barfoundation/application.asp)
	Amherst H. Wilder Foundation (http://www.wilder.org/)
	The McKnight Foundation (http://www.mcknight.org/)
	Minnesota State Department of Education (http://education.state.mn.us/MDE/Learning_Support/Counseling_Character_Service_Learning/Service_Learning/Grant_Applications_and_Awards/index.html)
Federal	Office of Juvenile Justice and Delinquency Prevention (OJJDP) (http://ojjdp.ncjrs.org/funding/FundingList.asp)
	U.S. Department of Education (including the Office of Special Education OSEP) (http://www.ed.gov/fund/grant/find/edlite-forecast.html)
Other	A research-based program provides a page with funding ideas http://www.cfchildren.org/support/funding/opps/

projects in the area), state (e.g., state department of education, other state entities) and federal levels (e.g., U.S. Department of Education, U.S. Department of Health and Human Services, Office of Juvenile Justice and Delinquency Prevention) (Raines & Alvarez, 2006). Examples of funders at each level are provided in Table 5.3. Note that some foundations allow for a common grant application that can be used to apply for funding from multiple foundations and is available from a state foundation organization.

Community-wide Collaboration

Many sources of funding require a multidisciplinary and multiagency approach to addressing the issue. Seeking grant funds to implement research-based programs is one way in which school districts can work with the local agencies to address a common issue. In some cases the fiscal agent for the grant must be a school district; in other cases it must be a community agency, and in other cases an institution of higher education. Collaborating on grant writing expands the availability of funds to address the problem because each entity has access to different funds that could be leveraged to address an issue. While schools might have access to Safe & Drug Free School dollars, a local agency may have funds to provide school-linked counseling services, or evaluation services. The literature emphasizes the need to collaborate with the community to produce good outcomes for students (DeSocio et al., 2007; McCluskey, Bynum, & Patchini, 2004; McCray, 2006).

Improving School Climate: A School-wide Tier I Approach

Utilizing the framework of Response to Intervention (RtI) is the first step in developing a comprehensive continuum of services to address early attendance issues. A comprehensive Tier 1 school-wide approach must be developed and serve as a strong foundation for interventions at the Tier 2 and Tier 3 levels. Without a strong foundation that addresses early intervention, strategies utilized at Tiers 2 and 3 will not produce good student outcomes.

Current research has demonstrated that comprehensive interventions to address truancy at school-wide, small group, and individual levels increases the likelihood of producing good student outcomes (Eaton, Brener, & Kann, 2008; U.S. Department of Education Institute of Educational Sciences, 2008). In an effort to begin to define behavioral expectations at the Tier 1 level, practitioners must first review research related to school engagement, a strong predictor of school attendance. The U.S. Department of Education, Institute of Education Sciences (2008) identifies indicators of school engagement as, "attendance, class participation, effort in doing schoolwork and avoidance of disciplinary actions (notably suspensions). . . [and] interest and enthusiasm, a sense of belonging, and identification with the school" (p. 5).

The National Center for School Engagement (NCSE) supports these indicators with the "three A's necessary for school success . . . attendance . . . attachment [to school] . . . achievement [academic]" (2009). Fantuzzo, Grim, and Hazan (2005) note best practices in truancy reduction as "the following: (a) a commitment from schools to keep at-risk youth in school, (b) collaboration with community resources, (c) a continuum of supports . . . (d) parent involvement, and (e) built-in capacity to conduct an ongoing evaluation of the intervention program" (p. 658).

In summary, research identifies indicators of school engagement as rate of attendance, grades, and level of involvement in school. The level of school commitment to engaging students includes measuring desire to keep students in schools, collaboration with community resources, and communication with parents. These indicators could be used as a baseline for attendance issues in a school building or district.

Tier I School-wide Interventions: Addressing Academic, Social, and Emotional Expectations

As noted previously, the literature on school improvement and truancy emphasizes the need for school-wide strategies to address issues in the school environment. It is clear in the research that school climate can impact attendance. Areas identified as important in assessing the school climate: (a) Attitudes of teachers and administrators, (b) consistent policies around attendance and truancy, and (c) school safety (DeSocio et al., 2006).

Attitudes of Teachers and Administrators

Based on a review of current research, the U.S. Department of Education Institute of Education Sciences (2008) recommends the development of a school climate that provides students with a sense of belonging and persona-lized encouragement (academic, social, behavioral) with special attention placed on transition years to middle school/junior high school and high school. The National Research Council Committee on Increasing High School Students' Engagement and Motivation to Learn (2004) states that "evidence suggests that student engagement and learning are fostered by a school climate characterized by an ethic of caring and supportive relationships, respect, fair-ness, and trusts; and teachers' sense of shared responsibility and efficacy related to student learning" (p. 103). This is important because when Attwood and Croll (2006) interviewed high school students that were truant, they found that "what was common to almost all the truants was that they had poor relationships with teachers" (p. 480). Poor relationships with teachers and administrators contribute to student nonattendance (Davies & Lee, 2006; Fallis & Opotow, 2003). In addition to the real or perceived attitudes of teachers and administrators, Dube and Orpinas (2009) found that "studies support the idea that the majority of children's attendance problems are positively reinforced. This finding is not surprising, given that previous studies have found that students often think that school is boring, classes are unengaging, and staff members are unapproachable, making absences more likely to occur" (p. 91–92). Baseline data about the students' perception of support from teachers and administrators should be collected and continuously measured to track improved school climate that facilitates student engagement.

Recognizing Good Attendance: Consistent Policies and Behavioral Expectations

It is important in Tier 1 to define the school-wide expectation for attendance. When does lack of attendance at school or missing a certain number of classes become an issue? The individual school must define these expectations for attendance, though district policy will guide the definition. In addition to identifying the behavioral expectation regarding attendance, clear procedures for addressing absences from school must be developed (or current policies revised based on the behavioral expectation). Evidence shows that truancy is more prevalent in schools that have inconsistent enforcement of truancy policy (Epstein & Sheldon, 2002; Teasley, 2004). As the table of state statutes in Chapter 2 shows, the definitions of truancy vary considerably. It is important for support staff to be familiar with the state statute to inform the benchmark used as the expected behavior.

Additional considerations in developing attendance benchmarks include the fact that research has identified issues of nonattendance visible as early as elementary school and shows the pattern of absences increasing over time (Lyon & Colter, 2007). However, at what point is nonattendance defined as a problem, or in the case of Response to Intervention in Tier 1, what is the benchmark or behavioral expectation for attendance that would trigger a need for a more intensive (Tier 2) intervention?

Efforts to identify this benchmark can be found in the literature. In 2000, Wisconsin changed the definition of truancy from five or more unexcused absences in 10 consecutive days or 10 per semester, to five unexcused absences per semester (Wisconsin Legislative Audit Bureau, 2000). Dube and Orpinas (2009) report that, "students are referred to the school social workers if unexcused absences continue. Typically between six and nine ... however, each school sets up its own criteria" (p. 88). Lyon and Colter (2007) suggest, "a cutoff of no more than 10% unexcused nonattendance over a period of up to 3 months be employed.... This period is long enough to establish a clear pattern of problematic nonattendance, but is still sensitive enough to identify low-level school-refusing" (p. 560).

With these suggestions in mind, each school building must review attendance data first for consistency of reporting, and then analyze it to see at what point, in their specific school, absences become more than that which is expected of 80%–90% of the students in their school. Once the benchmark is set for Tier 1, the process for following up on school absences and recording them in a consistent fashion is the next step (DeSocio et al., 2007). An example of decision-making criteria for one school district moving students from Tier 1 to Tier 2 can be found in Figure 5.1.

Decision Rules

80% Decision Rule: If less than 80% of students are not meeting benchmarks, review core program(s)

20% Decision Rule: Students below the 20th percentile in academic skills and/or with chronic behavior needs* are placed in small group instruction

Change Small Group or Individual Interventions Rule: When progress data is below aim-line on three (3) consecutive days, or when six (6) data points produce a flat or a decreasing trend-line

*More than 5 absences or more than 3 counselling or discipline referrals in a 30 day period

FIGURE 5.1. Decision-making Criteria for Tier 1 to Tier 2 Intervention.
Source: http://www.rti4success.org/images/stories/pdfs/lolich_data-based.pdf.

Consistency in tracking absences and applying interventions will increase the likelihood of improved school attendance. Addressing truancy requires this foundation to be laid, and while attendance issues will be addressed, the impact on the number of truants will not be seen for several years. Consistency at Tier 1 and the development of a benchmark behavior expectation related to attendance allows school personnel to identify which students might be in need of additional support at Tier 2 (see Chapter 6).

Other environmental factors that can impact the rate of attendance, especially at the middle school/junior high school or senior high school levels, include administrative decisions on structuring the offering of classes and supervision issues. The Wisconsin Legislative Audit Bureau (2000) notes:

> The use of a block schedule, rather than the more traditional hourly schedule has reduced truancy problems in some schools. . . . Block scheduling may reduce truancy rates because students may have an incentive to attend when more instruction time may be missed. Also, with fewer class periods, students are moving through the building fewer times, which gives them less opportunity to leave the building. (p. 16)

This same article suggests that attention be paid to allowing off-campus lunches and other transition times that could contribute to students leaving school for the day. Finally, a school climate audit would not be complete without examining student safety in school and walking or riding to/from school, which could impact student attendance. In fact, students often report being bullied on the way to/from school (Attwood & Croll, 2006).

Communication with Parents

Constant and consistent communication with parents regarding attendance is essential to involving the success of a plan to address the issue, including communication with families about all full days or partial days missed from school (Epstein & Sheldon, 2002). Parents should also be invited to participate on school and community committees that address the issue of truancy.

How Community Agencies Fit with Tier 1 of RtI

Support for collaborating with community agencies was provided earlier in this chapter. These collaborative opportunities include sharing resources, applying for grant funding, and sharing evaluation expertise. Not only do school districts and agencies recognize the importance of collaborating to address the issue, but policy makers have also recognized the importance of collaboration and leveraging resources (Epstein & Sheldon, 2002; Fantuzzo, Grim, & Hazan 2005; White, Fyfe, Campbell, & Goldkamp, 2001). Mogulescu & Segal (2002) developed a descriptive report of effective programs that address truancy. In their review they identified three important themes in developing a continuum of services to address all levels of attendance issues:

> First, all of these programs approach truancy prevention in a collaborative, multi-agency fashion. Jurisdictions taking a coordinated approach to truancy not only yield financially tenable outcomes, but also achieve better social outcomes for troubled youth. Second, all of the programs highlighted in this paper integrate the common expectation that schools take action in the first instance to identify patterns of absence, notify parents of the pattern, or attempt some school-based solutions before referring the child to the juvenile justice system. Finally, the programs across all three categories are built around the assumption that truancy is a symptom of more significant familial or emotional problems and seek to identify and address the environmental factors underlying the pattern of truancy. (Mogulescu & Segal, 2002, pp. 3–4)

The importance of collaboration is well documented; however, it is important to note that there are numerous articles involving punishment of the student and/or parents of students because of nonattendance. Practitioners should be cautioned that, 'court sanctions often fail to address the underlying issues facing families and preventing children from attending school' (Fantuzzo, Grim, & Hazan, 2005, p. 658). Other studies support this notion (Mogulescu & Segal, 2002); furthermore, Lyon and Colter (2007) state the following:

> Presently, school refusal research is full of biases that encourage subjectivity and, for many children, promote punitive tactics in the name of interventions.... Only by expanding samples, definitions, and attention to context in our assessment procedures can some of these biases be overcome so that children experiencing this problem may be properly identified and interventions can be applied in a manner more consistent with their needs. (p. 562)

In Tier 1, community agencies can support the implementation of school-wide programs by being invited to participate in the planning and implementation of the program, by supporting curriculum delivery in the classroom or other settings, or by participating in the review of program evaluation activities.

Role of Student Support Staff

Student services staff could be called on to use their skills and knowledge to chair committees that review, select, obtain buy-in, and implement a Tier 1 school-wide intervention that includes a behavioral expectation related to attendance. Knowledge of systems change will assist in working with school personnel who may be wary of implementing a new intervention in their classroom. Knowledge of policy development will enable student support services personnel to be instrumental in the review and potential revision of policies associated with attendance. Student services personnel should advocate for strengths-based interventions as opposed to the punitive approach to attendance and truancy that is prevalent in the literature and the state statutes. Student services personnel are adept at working collaboratively with other disciplines and other agencies and can serve as the contact person for community agencies interested in being involved with the development, implementation, and evaluation of a program that addresses attendance. Finally, assisting with the analysis and interpretation of the results and reporting program outcomes in a visual format are tasks that student services personnel have that can contribute to establishing and maintaining an effective system to address truancy.

Sample School-wide Programs That Promote Attendance

The sample programs presented in this chapter are school-based programs, but this is not intended to discount the role that community agencies can play in the successful implementation of school-based prevention and intervention. A brief description of two programs is provided as a sample for the reader with the knowledge that there are many more options for school-wide interventions that address attendance.

Positive Behavioral Interventions and Supports

Positive Behavioral Intervention and Supports (PBIS) is considered a research-based practice by all resources listed in this chapter. School-wide PBIS (SW-PBIS) provides a good structure to implement Tier 1 interventions. SW-PBIS is defined as "a decision making framework that guides selection, integration, and implementation of the best evidence-based practices for all students" (www. pbis.org/school/what_is_swpbs.aspx, 2009). SW-PBIS requires a school to:

- Develop a continuum of scientifically based behavior and academic interventions and supports
- Use data to make decisions and solve problems
- Arrange the environment to prevent the development and occurrence of problem behavior
- Teach and encourage prosocial skills and behaviors
- Implement evidence-based behavioral practices with fidelity and accountability
- Screen universally and monitor student performance & progress continuously (www.pbis.org/school/what_is_swpbs. aspx, 2009).

These are all best practices noted in the beginning of the chapter, however SW-PBIS provides the structure needed to develop a good Tier 1 foundation. Decision-making criteria related to attendance, and a clear link between function of the behavior and level of intervention required to meet the student's need. Many resources for implementing SW-PBIS are located on the website, including descriptions of PBIS at each Tier, PowerPoint presentations, research articles, and implementation checklists.

At the school-wide level, a team is developed (or an existing team used) to create three to five behavioral expectations for the entire school. In brief, a process is followed to clearly define the behavioral expectations in all school settings (e.g., library, cafeteria, recess, on the bus), develop clear and consistent procedures for students displaying behavior that does not meet expectations, identify methods of measuring the number of students meeting behavioral expectations, and frequently review and analyze data. A behavioral curriculum is utilized to reinforce expectations. A blueprint for implementation of SW-PBIS is available and includes a very detailed rubric for implementation (www. pbis.org/pbis_resource_detail_ page.aspx?Type=4&PBIS_ResourceID=223). The implementation of SW-PBIS as outlined in the blueprint has resulted in improved school climate and academic achievement. And a decrease in office referrals (Sailor et al., 2006).

As of October 2008, there were 31 states with a state-level implementation team that can provide training and coaching to schools or districts interested in SW-PBIS (Spaulding, Horner, May, & Vincent, 2008), limiting the cost of implementation. However, it is important to note, "successful large-scale implementation and large-scale sustainability of SW-PBIS requires a multi-year investment in systematic and comprehensive training, coaching, and evaluation" (Muscott, Mann, & LeBrun, 2008). The costs to implement SW-PBIS implementation is not as straightforward as providing a list of costs, due to the fact that SW-PBIS does not rely on a specific curriculum; rather, the brunt of the cost is quantified in time needed to implement SW-PBIS with fidelity and an investment of more than one school year to see results. In states where there is a state implementation team, training and coaching is available and could be provided through the state department of education. Most schools utilize the web-based School-wide Information System (SWIS) data-base to track data such as attendance and office referrals, which costs $250 per school building per year (SWIS, 2009). The cost of program curriculum implemented to teach skills related to behavioral expectations would be additional. Research-based programs such as Lions Quest, which is described below, can be integrated into SW-PBIS.

Lions Quest

Lions Quest, a program of the Lions Club International Foundation, is a comprehensive life skills education program designed for school-wide and classroom implementation with students age 6 to 17. Skills for Growing (SFG) targets students grades K-5, Skills for Adolescence (SFA) grades 6-8, and Skills for Action (SFC) grades 9-12. The goal of the program is to assist students in developing positive commitments to their families, schools, peers, and communities. Program facilitators are required to complete a two-day certification training (lions-quest.org). Depending on grade level between 24 and 102, 45-minute sessions are available.

Lions Quest teaches social/emotional skills that encourage good citizen-ship, strong character, and a commitment to helping others. The format of the curriculum includes presentations, discussions, group work, role-playing, service-learning, and reflection. Research on the program measured social functioning, success in school, behavior, and attitude toward alcohol and drugs. Program delivery has been studied in rural and urban schools with diverse populations that include American Indian, black or African American, Asian, and Hispanic or Latino students. Lions Quest has also been implemented in at least 30 countries and translated into 20 different languages. Training costs are $500 per person for a 2-day regional training (excluding the cost of travel and per diem). The curriculum must be purchased to attend the training (lions-quest.org). The curriculum is $99 to $120, student books that accompany the curriculum cost $2.50 to $5.95 per student. According to National Registry of Evidence-based Programs and Practices (2007a), program evaluation results indicate that:

> Participants averaged fewer days of absence in the full marking period following the intervention (p = .046)... Misconduct was measured through teachers' daily logs of individual students low-level aggressive acts (e.g., insubordination, verbal abuse, loitering or trespassing, ... truancy)... participants had half the number of negative behaviors in the intervention and follow-up periods compared with other students (p < .022)... participants also received comparatively lower misconduct ratings from their teachers during the intervention. (NREPP, 2009)

Districts considering the implementation of this program should consider cost of training, cost of the curriculum, length of time needed to deliver the curriculum, length of the program, and the need to evaluate outcomes for students and process outcomes for program delivery.

Conclusion

This chapter reviewed valuable resources needed to identify research-based programs that address nonattendance and truancy prevention; criteria to consider when selecting a program; creating readiness for program implementation; and two universal school-wide programs that can be implemented to address the Tier 1 behavioral expectation of attendance preventing future truancy. Emphasis was placed on involving community agencies and parents in the process of program selection, implementation, and evaluation. Additionally, it was noted that student support staff should take a strengths-based approach to addressing the issue of nonattendance/truancy in schools, as opposed to punitive measures. The next chapter will address Tier 2 targeted group and Tier 3 intensive, individual level interventions.

6

■ ■ ■

Best Practice in Truancy Prevention/Intervention: Tier 2 and Tier 3

Introduction

The previous chapter addressed the selection of evidence-based practices and the implementation of strategies to address attendance/truancy at the Tier 1 school-wide level. This chapter will address interventions at the Tier 2 targeted group and Tier 3 intensive individual levels. Attwood and Croll (2006) interviewed 15- and 16-year-old students with a history of truancy and found that "in just over half of the cases a *precipitating event* or series of connected events could be identified as the immediate explanation for a significant episode of truancy ... [and] For the young people for whom no clear precipitating event was apparent, substantial periods of truancy had followed on from a general disillusion with the school" (p. 479). Reid (2003) also found that "the initial cause or trigger point for the absence occurs when pupils are comparatively young, normally between the ages of seven and thirteen" (p. 355). Although Tier 1 interventions could address general disillusionment with school, specific precipitating events will most likely need to be addressed by Tier 2 targeted group or Tier 3 intensive individual interventions.

In Chapter 5, general information about developing a "norm" for the school-wide attendance rate was presented. The baseline is set at the attendance pattern of 80%-90% of students. A comprehensive and well-implemented school-wide program will result in improved school attendance for those students who make up the 80%-90%. Once the rate of attendance for 80%–90% of students is set, the criteria for a Tier 2 intervention based on attendance can be set. Figure 5.1 (Chapter 5) provides an example of the criteria for movement to Tier 2: "more than 5 absences ... in a 30-day period" (http://www.rti4success.org/images/stories/pdfs/lolich_data-based.pdf).

School-specific, clear criteria should be set, and then criteria for movement to Tier 3 should be developed. This framework assumes that the possibility of environmental conditions (e.g., classroom, school) triggering the behavior has been eliminated.

Tier 2 Targeted Group Interventions

Multidisciplinary Assessment

Students who do not meet the school-wide expectation related to attendance must then be considered for a Tier 2 intervention. Data collected in Tier 1 will inform student services personnel about the frequency and duration of days missed from school, and in some cases the reason for the absence. However, the need to collect further data to select a targeted group intervention best suited to the student is necessitated. Kearney and Bates (2005) suggest, "As a general rule, a multimethod, multisource assessment approach is recommended for this population given the tremendous behavioral variability often presented" (p. 208). The value of collecting data from multiple sources is corroborated by the literature (Kearney, Lemons, & Silverman, 2004; Reid, 2003). Kearney and Bates (2005) also note, "Behavioral observations are . . . useful for youth with school refusal behavior. Specific protocols for conducting such observations generally call for detailed descriptions and ratings of a child's behavior in the morning before going to school" (p. 208). Other recommendations in the literature for points of observation include, "days when his or her parents accompany or not accompany the child to school . . . and during the school day" (Kearney, Lemons, & Silverman, 2004, p. 280). These multiple points of observation provide detail to complete a functional behavior assessment (FBA).

Assessment of the function of attendance issues can be conducted utilizing a Functional Behavior Assessment. An FBA is an assessment tool normally utilized in assessing a special education student's behavior to ascertain the reason a student engages in a certain behavior. School districts already have in place a format for conducting FBAs. However, broader application of this tool is recommended for use with all students exhibiting behaviors that impact academic progress. The rigor of the FBA at Tier 2 will be less intensive than one completed at Tier 3 (Braaksma Fynaardt & Richardson, in press).

Dube and Orpinas (2009) state, "Findings from the present study suggest that school refusal is a complex problem that may require interventions targeted at the underlying factors that motivate absenteeism" (p.94). Several researches support understanding of attendance issues based on the function of the behavior (Kearney, 2007; Kearney, Lemons, & Silverman 2004; Teasley, 2004). Researchers note that the functional reason for nonattendance remains consistent over time (Kearney, 2007) and, if not addressed, increases in frequency (DeSocio et al., 2007). Therefore, addressing the function of the behavior is more likely to produce a reduction in truancy. Tier 2 interventions groups together students with common functions of the behavior related to attendance. Students continue to receive Tier 1 schoolwide interventions simultaneously with Tier 2 interventions.

Progress Monitoring

In addition to baseline student data collected during Tier 1 and that collected during the assessment for Tier 2 services, the response to the targeted group intervention should be documented and reviewed regularly to ensure a positive response to the intervention (Kearney & Bates, 2005). This is because "Decisions about treatment options should rest on empirical data about a given case—in particular, the form and function of a child's behavior" (Kearney & Bates, 2005, p. 212). At Tier 2, decisions are based on a combination of response to the targeted group intervention and continued monitoring of the Tier 1 behavior expectations to watch for improvement.

Involving Students and Parents in Problem Solving

As in Tier 1, continued contact with the family on a regular basis in addition to interventions with the student will promote better behavioral outcomes (Kearney & Bates, 2005). Parents are informed about the Tier 2 intervention, and in many cases there is a complimentary program component made available to them (e.g., parent workshop, parenting group). The student is involved in a targeted group intervention, which allows them to problem solve with their peers and a program facilitator. The problem solving should address the function of the behavior.

Role of Support Staff

Selecting research-based interventions in Tier 2 should follow the same process as that described in Chapter 5. The intervention will have among its primary goals improving attendance and addressing the function of behaviors associated with nonattendance. The functions of the behavior will vary among educational levels and among students. Student support services personnel should play a primary role in developing criteria for students needing Tier 2 interventions, selecting and implementing interventions with fidelity, monitoring the progress of students, and involving families in the process.

Nonattendance can be prompted or exacerbated by many issues (e.g., family issues, alcohol/drug use); however, interventions at the Tier 2 and Tier 3 levels may have originally been developed to address these related issues, and results indicate a positive impact on attendance. Also, programs implemented at the Tier 1 level may have components that simultaneously provide a Tier 2 intervention. Therefore, although sample programs have a Tier 1 component, only Tier 2 strategies of the programs will be discussed in the next section. Student services staff will be involved in program implementation at all tiers of intervention.

Early Risers Skills for Success

Early Risers Skills for Success is a research-based program listed on the National Registry of Evidence-based Programs and Practices (NREPP, 2007b). This program targets older elementary level students ages 6 to 12. Despite targeting behaviors that place students at risk for substance use or mental health issues, this program has been used successfully in improving attendance in a truancy prevention project (NREPP, 2007b).

Program components include student and family activities facilitated by a program specific staff member called a "family advocate." The student-centered strategies include a summer day camp, after school friendship groups during the academic year to expand on learning during summer camp, case management, and mentoring. Strategies to work with families include evening activities held at the school, parenting education, and supportive case management. Because the core of the program targets a group of students as opposed to an individual student, Early-Risers is considered a Tier 2 intervention.

Program evaluation studies have demonstrated positive outcomes in the areas of academic achievement (which includes attendance), behavioral self-regulation, social skills, and relationship with parent (NREPP, 2007b). This program has been studied in rural and urban school settings.

Costs associated with implementing the program include a two-day onsite training, which costs approximately $7,000 and includes the costs of five manuals, permission to reproduce forms, and some level of ongoing technical assistance following the training. Curriculum costs are separate from the training, and the program suggests hiring a program facilitator, which results in an estimated cost of $1,500 to $2,500 per student (NREPP, 2007b).

Research comparing implementation of the program to a control group reveals outcomes that include academic improvement, improvement in behavior self-regulation of students with more severe behavior issues, improvement in social competence, and increased use of effective discipline methods by parents to address the behavior of the more severely aggressive students (NREPP, 2007b). The curriculum includes an implementation manual, an instrument to assist with measuring the fidelity of the implementation, and program satisfaction surveys (NREPP, 2007b).

Achievement for Latinos Through Academic Success (ALAS)

ALAS was rated as an effective research-based program by the What Works Clearinghouse in 2006 and noted as a promising practice by the Promising Practices Network (PPN, 2009). ALAS is targeted to Latino students, with and without disabilities, in middle/junior high school (NSET, 2009). This program includes monitoring attendance, a 10-week problem-solving curriculum, frequent academic updates to parents and students about student progress, parent training, social activities, and links to community resources (NDPC, 2009; WWC, 2006a). This program is a Tier 2 intervention because it targets students who have been identified during the year prior to entry into middle/junior high school utilizing a 6-item rating scale (WWC, 2006a), and the program is targeted at a group of students rather than an individual student. The program should be delivered over a period of three years or the duration of middle/junior high school; however, monitoring of students' response to this intervention must determine students' continued participation. The program was researched in urban schools with Latino students with and without disabilities (NDPC, 2009; WWC, 2006a). Staff hired for program implementation facilitates the program and according to WWC (2006a) the cost to implement ALAS was $1,185 in 2005.

Coca-Cola Valued Youth Program

The Intercultural Development Research Association located in Texas developed the Coca-Cola Valued Youth Program (VYP). While this program is a promising practice with some research to support it, WWC (2009) indicates some concern about the research base for this program, stating,

> No studies of the *Coca-Cola Valued Youth Program* that fall within the scope of the Dropout Prevention review protocol meet What Works Clearinghouse (WWC) evidence standards. The lack of studies meeting WWC evidence standards means that, at this

time, the WWC is unable to draw any conclusions based on research about the effectiveness or ineffectiveness of the *Coca-Cola Valued Youth Program*. (WWC, 2009).

There are many promising practices that do not have the level of research integrity needed to meet criteria for reviewing organizations. Practitioners should take this into consideration when selecting a program for their school and consider contributing to the research base of promising practices, such as this program.

The research for this program was originally funded by Coca-Cola, hence its inclusion in the name of the program. This program targets middle/junior high and high school students with the goal of improving basic academic skills, self-perception, and school attendance. The interesting "twist" (IDRA, 2009) is that students that are experiencing academic, disciplinary, and nonattendance problems are trained to be tutors for students at least four years younger.

Program components include a weekly class for the tutors to enhance their tutoring skills, paid time tutoring younger students four hours per week, educational field trips, recognition of accomplishments, and meetings with an adult mentor (IDRA, 2009). This research-based program includes a comprehensive program evaluation plan that involves formally observing tutors working with the younger students, pre– and post–academic year teacher surveys, tutor interviews, and parent surveys (IDRA, 2009).

IDRA provides interested schools with an implementation booklet on their website and describes the cost of implementation and information about potential funding sources that can be valuable for this program and similar ones. The booklet can be found at www.idra.org/Coca-Cola_Valued_Youth_Program. html/Getting_Started_at_Your_School/.VYP is considered a Tier 2 intervention because the program is provided to a group of students that are at-risk for a variety of reasons, as opposed to an intervention with one individual student. Students' response to this intervention should be monitored throughout the program.

WhyTry

Another promising practice is WhyTry, a program developed for students in grades K-12 that uses a multisensory approach to motivate students to succeed in the acquisition of life skills. The program was developed to address issues related to attendance, behavior, substance abuse, and low academic achievement (WhyTry, 2009). The curriculum has 10 units covering topics such as resisting peer pressure, decision making, problem solving, building a support network, and motivation to succeed. The skill taught in each unit is reinforced with a visual analogy, music, physical movement, and experiential activities. The curriculum is delivered over a period of 20 weeks. WhyTry can be easily used at all three levels of the Response to Intervention tiers. However, at the Tier 2 level, it is a targeted group intervention for students needing more intense and frequent interventions. Several small studies have examined the efficacy of the WhyTry program showing positive results in a range of student outcomes. Students who completed the WhyTry program showed an improved grade point average, fewer absences, and increased levels of graduation than did students in the control group (Bushnell & Card, 2003; Eggett 2003). Research continues on outcomes of this program.

Training in the WhyTry curriculum is conducted over two days and is offered at different locations across the United States. The cost of attending a 2-day training workshop is $550 per person and includes the full curriculum. Onsite training is also available. In addition, each student participating in the program will need a $10 journal (WhyTry, 2009).

Tier 3 Intensive Individual Interventions

About 5% of students do not respond to Tier 1 and Tier 2 interventions, in which case Tier 3 interventions need to be added. Monitoring the student's progress in response to the other interventions is used to support the decision to add intensive individualized interventions. Further assessment of the student is required. At the Tier 3 level of intervention, it is important to select an intervention that addresses the root of the problem. Functional behavior assessments are being used in general education to assist student services personnel in identifying the function of behaviors such as skipping or missing school/classes. Studies have demonstrated that the intervention strategies that most closely address the function of a behavior are the most effective methods of decreasing the incidence of unwanted behaviors (Ellingson et al., 2000; Ingram, Lewis-Palmer, & Sugai, 2005; Meyer, 1999; Repp, Felce, & Barton, 1998). In fact, Lyon and Colter (2007) found that "intervention programs for truancy often fail to consider the specifics of each child's condition in a manner that is clinically meaningful ... [applying] the same intervention steps to all participants" (p. 554). Lyon and Colter (2007) state, "it is essential that these interventions are driven by a clear understanding of the origins and maintenance of school refusal behavior" (p. 562). Teasley (2004) notes that "school social workers should determine individual causality of truancy before developing an intervention plan" (p. 122).

Assessment

Assessment at Tier 3 requires a more in-depth view of the root of the problem: attendance. Braaksma Fynaardt and Richardson (in press) note:

> A more rigorous FBA will usually include more formal interviews with multiple people (e.g., general education teacher, specials teachers, parent(s), and student), direct observations of the student in multiple settings across multiple days, and may also include more formal assessments of student skills. (p. 151)

In some research studies that address truancy and related issues, individuals were assessed utilizing the School Refusal Assessment Scale for Children (SRAS-C) (Kearney, 2007). Interestingly, the SRAS-C is very similar to an FBA because it was developed based on the functional model of school refusal behavior that explores why a child is not attending school (avoidance, escape, attention, or a tangible reimbursement) (Dube & Orpinas, 2009; Kearney, Lemons, & Silverman 2004).

Mentoring

Based on a review of current research, the U. S. Department of Education Institute of Education Sciences (2008) recommends assigning an adult to students to develop a "meaningful and sustained personal relationship with a trained adult" (p. 17) (USDE IES, 2008). This recommendation is supported by DeSocio et al. (2007) in a literature review on engaging students who are truant. They found that utilization of a mentor promotes engagement with the school, identifying this as a best practice. Teasley (2004) notes that, "mentoring has ... proven to be a useful method for reducing truancy rates and appears to be one of increasing merit" (p. 122). McCray (2006) suggests that mentors assigned to work with students should not already be authority figures in the student's life.

Involving Students and Parents in Problem Solving

Addressing family simultaneously can help address issues that are impacting attendance. In Tier 3, the work is conducted with a specific family to assist an individual student in addressing issues related to attendance. For example, when a mentor is utilized, student services personnel could simultaneously work with family members to problem-solve issues related to the student's attendance.

Role of Support Staff

The role of student support services personnel is to identify individualized intensive interventions that are specific to the student, implement or assist with implementation, monitor student response to the intervention, and review progress to ensure the intervention is effective. Generally, student services staff are familiar and most comfortable with this level of service provision. However, monitoring the effectiveness of the intervention may not have been a part of their role up to this point. Another task is continuous communication with parents and administrators about student progress.

Check & Connect

Check & Connect is a program that focuses on increasing students' engagement in school by targeting risk factors that can be altered such as tardiness, skipping class, nonattendance, office referrals, and suspensions (Evelo et al., 1996). The program has been rated for its effectiveness by the What Works Clearinghouse (WWC, 2006b) and has shown positive outcomes with students related to both staying in and progressing in school. The program manual provides a list of criteria for selecting students that will best respond to the intervention and suggests monitoring these same behaviors throughout the intervention to assess the student's progress. Each student is assigned a monitor who is responsible for communicating with teachers, parents, and others about the student's progress in school, assessing the student's level of engagement in school, and creating a plan based on that to strengthen engagement (Evelo et al., 1996). Evelo and others (1996) note that "What is required from a monitor are the following skills and attitudes: persistence, belief that all kids have abilities, willingness to work closely with families . . ., [and] advocacy skills" (p. 7). The intent is for a monitor to work with a student for more than one academic year to provide continuity for the student, even if the student changes schools within a district.

Interventions provided by the monitor are documented to track student progress and ensure fidelity of program implementation. Interventions include problem-solving conversations about the value of staying in school, academic support, and links to community activities. The interventions can increase in intensity as the needs are assessed. Talking points are provided to the monitor for many scenarios they may face with the student, along with procedures to deal with incidents such as suspensions.

Curriculum training for Check & Connect is provided in Minneapolis, Minnesota, at a cost of $545, which includes the cost of an implementation manual. On-site training is also available by contacting the program developers at checkandconnect@umn.edu. Although program training is recommended, the implementation manual may be purchased for $45. The following is a case study that provides a more personal view of the impact of Check & Connect at the Tier 3 level.

Case Study: A Check & Connect Student

By Gale Mason-Chagil, Ph.D., with support from the Bush Foundation, Saint Paul, MN

Kisha (a pseudonym) was an African American young woman in the 9th grade in a Minneapolis Public High School who had low attendance and grades. Some of her problems with school stemmed from problems at home. For example, about halfway through the school year, her mother was physically abused by a domestic partner. The Monitor explained, "Kisha couldn't focus at all on her school work because she was just worried that this guy was coming back for her mom." He threatened the family several times and social services finally succeeded in obtaining a restraining order against the abuser. An observer commented: "They didn't know to what lengths he was going to go. So they have come out of a shelter and finally have been able to stabilize and rent this apartment. Then they're trying to decide, 'Do we stay here? He knows we live here. Or do we go back into the shelter?'"

Another problem for Kisha occurred when she fell and broke a bone during the second quarter. She said, "I wasn't coming to school. I was in and out of the hospital" and she fell behind on her schoolwork. Finally, Kisha started to make, "her own bad decisions, putting herself in dangerous places with dangerous people and doing the wrong things," explained the Monitor. "She failed everything second quarter . . . attendance was bad. Bad decisions, running away a lot;" substance use and sexual activity contributed to an unhealthy lifestyle. "Her mom isn't really parenting in a real active way. She feels helpless and doesn't really know what to do, so she's just letting Kisha run as she pleases in and out of the house. Not that she likes the behavior," said the Monitor.

Combined with all the other challenges in her life, Kisha was transitioning into high school. She said that the high school was bigger, had "more kids," and "there's more stuff you have to do," as compared to her former middle school. She explained: "You have more work you have to do in high school than in middle school, something that you've got to turn in. In middle school they give you an assignment, they don't really have a date you have to turn it in or whatever like that; you just turn it in whenever you want to turn it in. But at high school you've got to turn it in when they tell you to turn it in and how to turn it in or you're not going to get no grade. You will fail." According to Kisha, the hardest part about high school was, [trying to keep my grades up" after she got behind in her work. In the fall, when her mother was attacked and she had her injury, her grades were Ds and Fs.

Kisha and the Monitor developed a trusting relationship. Kisha's mother commented, "My daughter loves to talk to her. She doesn't like to talk to anyone but the Monitor." Also, she said, "Kisha she is not going to let too many people get into her business and get close to her, and then I seen she was working with the Monitor. I think the Monitor is a wonderful person. I am just grateful." Kisha mentioned that if it were not for the Monitor she would not talk with any adult in the school about barriers to her education. She said the Monitor was: "somebody I look up to, like I wouldn't trust nobody else but there's somebody I really like because she's like a real nice caring person. That's the only person I trust out of this whole entire school. . . . I don't trust nobody else. . . . If the Monitor is not there, I'm just going to have to wait until she get there. . . . if I get mad she say the right things to calm me down. She like, 'You have to think about the other person's feelings. How would it affect you if you was to do this and how would it affect you if you was to do that?'"

Through this trusting relationship, the Monitor mentored and advocated for Kisha. Kisha described ways that the Monitor helped her: "We sit and we talk and stuff about what I be doing. She came up with a game called 'Good Decision, Bad Decision.' It's like she gave you a situation and you need to tell her is it a good decision or a bad decision. You got to say why is it a good decision or a bad decision and how should you deal with it. . . . Like I ran away from home one time and she was trying to figure out why I did it. She was like, 'Running away from home and not going to school—good decision, bad decision?' I said that's a bad decision. She's like, 'Why?' Because I'm not going to school and I'm not learning nothing and I'm getting behind. She's like, 'good.'"

The Monitor located social services, including counseling related to the violence Kisha experienced in her home, and located other programs that provided support and structure for her when she was not at school. For example, the Monitor explained: "We signed her up for a community-based program so that she can meet an adult mentor who would really focus on her during that time and it could be twice a week—it's pretty intensive in the beginning, so I thought it would be good for the summer months when she doesn't have a lot of structure."

A key aspect to the relationship was that the Monitor monitored Kisha's academic progress and took steps to support her academic success. Kisha explained: "She look at my grades and then we'll pull up my attendance every once in awhile. If it's bad, I have to stay in school. If it's good, I keep doing the good work. Then with my grades, so if I had an F, well, she says, 'You have to go to your classes to get your work. You don't want to get behind.' So I have to go do what she says. Then we come together at the end of the day and figure out, 'How you going to keep these grades up?' She's a good person. I really like her."

The Monitor noted that Kisha was a good candidate for a new program in the school that was designed for students who were not doing well in mainstream classes. The Monitor, who regularly worked with this program because many of her students were part of the program, facilitated Kisha's enrollment. The program

Truancy Prevention and Intervention

offered smaller class sizes and more teacher attention, and additionally the Monitor tutored Kisha when necessary. Kisha said that when grades came out: "I'm thinking I didn't have good grades so when that progress report came, I was so happy. I cried. I actually cried because I couldn't believe I went from all Fs to like all Cs. I was so happy on that progress.... I'm trying to work hard now." The Monitor also helped Kisha earn credits so that she is on track to graduate. For example, Kisha was completing an on-line algebra course after school during the site visits. "She'll stay in the library with me and she has an algebra course that she can work through on line. If she finishes it, she'll get a credit for that," explained the Monitor.

The Monitor also helped Kisha sign up for summer school: "Maybe she's short one class but fourth quarter hasn't ended yet and fourth quarter looks like we're nose-diving here. So might as well get her signed up for that one class and if she needs any more, then she could go. That's another kind of structure [that is good] for her in the summer." Kisha and the Monitor also talked about her long-term education and career goals. Kisha said, "I signed up for Technical College. I signed up for the summer program. I signed up for something else.... For the summer and next year. Then the Monitor's trying to get me ready for college.... So I'm trying to go to college."

All of the key informants agreed that Kisha benefited greatly from the social and academic support that she gained through the trusting relationship with the Monitor. The Monitor was asked to reflect on what would have happened to Kisha if Check and Connect did not exist and she said, "I don't think she'd have the credits she has now if somebody wasn't chasing her." Kisha's mother commented, "My baby girl would not be in school today" if the Monitor was not there. Kisha said without the Monitor she would: "not be going to class, not doing my work like I used to, not getting as good grades as I get because that was kind of rough without the Monitor. I wasn't doing it; I was never in class, I never did my work until the Monitor came along. She's like 'If you don't do this, if you don't be in school, I'll truant you'.... It was like if I don't do this, there's always a consequence behind it, so dang, come on now. She's extra strict, so she's like a role model. I look up to her." Kisha continued: "I thought if I wasn't really working with her and she didn't push me as much as she did, I probably wouldn't be where I'm at now. I'd probably be like the way I used to be . . . second quarter wasn't so hot. Third quarter when I saw my grades after I started working with the Monitor, I was so happy. . . . I had an A in writing, a B+ in reading. . . . I wouldn't even have half of the credits I have now. I'd probably have like six or five."

Finally, Kisha explained why she thought the money to support Check and Connect should be continued: "I would tell them they should keep the money because it's so much help to some kids, not just me but like probably affect other kids too. So if they would not fund the Check and Connect program, some of these kids would probably be so behind. They wouldn't be on track [to graduate]. They'd probably be all behind. Check and Connect, they check with you and connect with you in different ways. If other students don't have nobody to check with them and try to come up with plans with them or what not, it would be useless. They wouldn't have no help. They wouldn't have nobody there for them like my Monitor is and everybody else from Check and Connect. . . . Everything was so hard but then you have a person like my Monitor in your life, she make things so easy like peaches and cream . . . that's what I'd tell them."

Not only did the Monitor create a supportive relationship with Kisha she also developed a close relationship with her mother. Even though the two women had never met, they regularly talked candidly on the phone, and the Monitor offered Kisha's mother advice on how to cope with challenges.

Despite all her work with Kisha, the Monitor worried about Kisha continuing with school. "Actually she's one I really still worry about for dropping out because she's 16 as a freshman and down on credits already and all this other life stuff going on around it. I still worry," said her Monitor. During her 10th grade year, Kisha moved to another Minneapolis high school. Check and Connect is now in all comprehensive high schools in Minneapolis. Therefore, soon after she transferred, a Check and

Connect Monitor in her new school communicated with Kisha. Kisha commented that her new Monitor was always checking up on her, "She stays on your tail. I cannot make a move—'aren't you supposed to be in this class? Aren't you supposed to be in that class? Where are you going?' ... she's right there. ... Gets me motivated." (May 26, 2009)

Conclusion

This chapter reviewed interventions at Tier 2 Targeted Group and Tier 3 Intensive Individual that address the issue of attendance/truancy. Emphasis was placed on the importance of identifying the root of the problem and the use of a functional behavior assessment as a valuable tool to do so. Sample programs at the Tier 2 level were described and a sample Tier 3 intervention with case study provided.

7

■ ■ ■

Case Example of the Role of School Social Workers in a Truancy Reduction Program: South Carolina Truancy Pilot

Introduction

This chapter examines a truancy reduction initiative in the Berkeley County School District (BCSD), located near coastal South Carolina (SC). It discusses the process of community collaboration, program design and evaluation, and the use of school social workers as team members for program intervention. Additionally, this chapter provides sample forms and examples that offer a model for a truancy reduction program[1].

Funding

The South Carolina Department of Education (SCDOE) received funding from the U.S. Department of Justice to develop the South Carolina Truancy and Dropout Prevention Initiative, a statewide strategic effort to curtail school dropouts, court appearances, and the secure confinement of status offenders. This dropout initiative was also intended to enhance truancy reduction efforts in our state. With those funds, the SCDOE established the South Carolina Truancy and Dropout Prevention Center to:

- Promote accurate processing and tracking of truancy and other status offenses
- Serve as a clearinghouse on effective research-based strategies and programs addressing truancy and dropout prevention.

[1] Appreciation is expressed to Phyliss Thornthwaithe, Coordinator for Children at Risk, Berkeley County School District, and Mary Ann Joseph, Conflict Solutions, Georgetown, South Carolina, for their collaboration in the Truancy Pilot and their assistance with this chapter.

- Assist communities by providing tools and resources needed to implement and sustain effective, research-based truancy and dropout prevention programs and strategies.

Activities were guided by a state multi-agency, interdisciplinary Truancy Steering Committee. This group was responsible for policy recommendations and oversight of the distribution of discretionary grants to school districts.

The SCDOE targeted school districts with the highest truancy rates, and requests for proposals were sent to those school districts. Berkeley County School District was fortunate to receive discretionary grant funding for three years. This discretionary grant was supplemented by a targeted grant from the same source directed through the South Carolina Department of Health and Environmental Control (DHEC). The targeted grants were given to three public health regions and their respective five school districts. These districts/schools were selected based on established criteria including high incidence of truancy and poverty as well as the lack of school social workers who specifically addressed school attendance. BCSD was one of the districts to enter into a memorandum of agreement (MOA) with DHEC Region 5 to pilot public health social workers for truancy prevention and intervention within the schools.

BCSD contracted with DHEC Region 5 for the services of two licensed social workers with master's degrees in social work (MSW) as well as training in public health to address the attendance and truancy problems in two BCSD middle schools. These social workers brought a biopsychosocial perspective to individual practice as well as population-based experience for the community and systems (macro) issues. They were well prepared by education and experience to work with individual students, their families, school personnel, and community representatives, and they had skills in writing treatment plans and program and community development.

Blueprint/MOA for Partnership

The following summary outlines the specifics of the MOA between DHEC Region 5 and the BCSD.

The partnership between DOE, BCSD, and DHEC Region 5 provided financial support for the services of two public health social workers in each of two middle schools as a demonstration of the effectiveness of social work services directed toward truancy and dropout prevention. The partnership's goal was to address the comprehensive health/mental health needs of children and families to promote school success to be measured by:

- Improved student attendance
- Improved student behavior in school
- Improved student grades
- Student access to medical care (connection to a medical home)
- Reduced student dropouts

The activities of the South Carolina–licensed MSW public health social worker included the following:

- Work within school population to reduce truancy and dropout behavior.
- Assist with securing a medical home for all students (primary care physician and dentist).
- Psychosocial assessment of student/family.
- Home visits or visits to parent/guardians' workplace.
- Mutually agreed upon goals (time limited, measurable, and outcome-based).
- Individual counseling.
- Family counseling.
- Group classes/counseling.
- Referral for additional resources.
- Staff education/consultation.
- Developing community participation and initiatives to curtail truancy.
- Program evaluation.
- Others as identified by school or district circumstances and program development needs.

School social workers developed individualized intervention/treatment plans with truant students and, at the same time, worked to connect them to the life of the school. They helped the school connect with students by working to ensure that the culture of the school was welcoming and supportive of all students. Strong scientific evidence demonstrates that increased student connection to school promotes improved educational motivation and classroom engagement, and not surprisingly, improved classroom attendance (Lehr, Sinclair, & Christenson, 2004). Additionally, school social workers coordinated with school personnel to track and evaluate a student's progress or recidivism once he or she successfully completed the intervention plans. Evaluation results were used to strengthen program structure and interventions and generalize lessons learned for application to truancy interventions across the state.

Resources provided by DHEC in support of partnership included the following:

- Personnel management.
- Professional supervision of social worker.
- Quality assurance of social work services.
- In-service training for social worker.
- Access to other health department services such as nursing, nutrition, and health education.

Resources provided by school district in support of school social work services included the following:

- On site supervision.
- Administrative support as indicated.
- Office space, supplies.
- Consultation/program development.
- Joint training to attendance officers and school social workers.

BCSD is the fourth largest school district in the state, with approximately 28,000 students. It is located approximately 40 miles from downtown Charleston, South Carolina. It is geographically one of the largest school districts in South Carolina. The district population is diverse, with approximately 46% African American students, 46% Caucasian students, and 8% students of other races. There are 37 schools in the district, each with many needs. Because the district is so large, a decision was made to focus on two of the most challenging schools, each located in low socioeconomic communities. The two middle schools selected, Berkeley Middle School with 1200 students and Sedgefield Middle School with 800 students, both qualify for Title I services due to the large number of students eligible for free or reduced lunch. At the time of the initial grant, BCSD employed three additional social workers; each had a caseload of about 10 to 13 schools. They were responsible for meeting the needs of students in these schools, but were not assigned to regularly address truancy issues.

Program Planning/Implementation

In 2005–06, two schools within the district were chosen to participate based on identified truancy rates. In 2006–07, work continued at Berkeley Middle

School and Sedgefield Middle School. An initial period of assessment was necessary, to meet with these schools to define and assess their process for identifying and intervening with truant students and their families. It was important to know what was currently being done in each school and what could be done to improve the process. During initial meetings, it became evident that the staff in the identified schools felt ill-prepared to implement the new state attendance statute and regulations, passed as a response to the federal No Child Left Behind Act. Attendance and truancy issues are governed by the South Carolina Code of Laws, Sections 59-65-10 through 59-65-280, and the South Carolina Code of Regulations, Reg. 43-274. The regulation uses a three-tiered approach for defining the varying levels of truant behavior. According to these regulations, students are defined as "truant" when they are 6 to 17 years of age and have three *consecutive* unlawful absences or a *total* of five unlawful absences. When students are truant, school staff are required to meet with the parent and student to develop a plan to improve attendance, referred to as an Attendance Intervention Plan (AIP). The school social worker assumed this role in the pilot.

A "Habitual Truant" is a student 12 to 17 years of age who fails to comply with the intervention plan and accumulates *two or more additional* unlawful absences. A "Chronic Truant" is a student between the ages of 12 to 17 who has been placed on "Order to Attend" and *accumulates additional* unlawful absences. "The varying levels of truancy are important because there are requirements and limitations at each level for what should and can be done to address the child's truant behavior" (Children's Law Office, 2006, p.7).

Staff discomfort with the new regulations was evident in the number of truants who had not been identified in the attendance database (SASI) and did not have an AIP in place, as required by the new South Carolina regulations. Attendance staff also believed there was a lack of human resources to address the problem. School attendance staff saw the problem as quite overwhelming since in the past, more often than not, there had been few consequences to the student when truancy cases were submitted to DJJ for case work-up and referral to the Solicitor's Office. School staff reported long delays before cases were heard, sometimes as long as one year or more.

It appeared that the Solicitor's Office placed little priority on truancy cases. The social workers felt that successful truancy intervention programs should include rewards for increased attendance as well as sanctions for continued truancy. It became apparent that the schools did not have a clearly defined process to address the truancy problems. We needed to form a step-by-step procedure to address truancy. Questions that needed answers included the following: Do we send a letter, or call the parent/s? Do we call the student? Who is responsible for contacting the parent or the child: the teachers or the administration? Who is responsible for determining why the child was not attending? How do we acknowledge/identify them as truant in the School Administration Student Information System (SASI)? How do we record attempts to intervene and intervention meetings?

Early in the process, the school social workers identified the attendance clerks as "vital" to the new system's success. They were brought into the system as key participants through: (a) School-level team-building between the social worker and attendance clerks (accountability), and (b) Annual training at the district level for all attendance clerks and social workers. As attendance clerks were brought into the process, they proposed a change in their job title. They suggested the need for more perceived authority for their role in truancy prevention. The school social workers helped to successfully advocate for the change. The title of attendance clerk was changed to attendance "officer," which did a great deal to improve morale among the staff and promoted a new respect from parents for the role the staff performed.

The training manual developed by Conflict Solutions (Joseph, 2006) was refined to reflect the new system that was put into place through the collaborative efforts of the Attendance Conciliation Team (ACT). Involving and asking for input from the attendance clerks, social workers, district staff, and ACT members ensured that the training manual accurately reflected the needs of its users, and promoted the buy-in from all levels necessary for success. The truancy identification and intervention process was easy to follow and the forms were more user-friendly. The success of the annual training held as in-service became evident in the annual decrease in the number of truants, the annual increase in the number of truants identified with intervention plans, and the increase in appropriate referrals to ACT.

In looking for positives of the current situation, we realized some of the schools were using a software program called *In Touch*. This program was designed for parents to look at their child's attendance, grades, homework assignments, and so forth. Schools that used the program thought it was very useful for staff and helpful for parents. The program was purchased for several of the high schools. A brochure was also developed that not only addressed the law, but also provided tips for parents to recognize signs of truancy. In addition, the district developed a simple one-page handout defining excused and unexcused absences and resulting truancy, in both

English and Spanish. This was the beginning of a systemic process, a step-by-step procedure, to address students with three consecutive or five total unexcused absences.

The key to any successful pilot is finding that "sparkplug" individual who believes in the cause and is in a position to make some things happen. A true advocate was found in Phyliss Thornthwaite, BCSD's Coordinator of Students at Risk programs. While the real need of the district was to increase the accuracy of reporting or face loss of state and federal dollars under the No Child Left Behind Act (NCLB), it was also understood that truancy is often the red flag for other issues that prevent educational success for students within the district.

School social workers began work on this effort during the 2006–07 school year. As they began to work in the schools, the district realized they had been working in a vacuum with little support to address the social issues that affect the community. Social workers recognized that if the system is not working, their best-practice interventions with students and families would be more difficult, possibly futile. It was at this point that the community came to the rescue.

To support the work of the two social workers and the school community, funds were used to secure the services of Conflict Solutions, a private mediation-consulting firm, directed by Mary Ann Joseph. Conflict Solutions was founded in 2000 with the primary purpose of working with schools and community-based organizations to effectively address issues that negatively impact student success. This collaboration has resulted in the development of two comprehensive truancy reduction/intervention programs that have been successfully implemented in five South Carolina School Districts.

Attendance Improvement Mediation (AIM) is a collaborative process designed to help families and schools address attendance problems with the help of a neutral third party—a trained mediator—in a neutral setting. The mediator helps the school team; the social worker and family identify the root causes of truancy and then develop an action plan to address those issues. The goals of the AIM program are to reduce the number of unlawful absences by identifying and addressing the root issues affecting attendance, to build communication and strengthen relationships between families and schools, and to identify systemic issues that negatively affect attendance so they can be addressed on a community-wide level.

The Attendance Conciliation Team (ACT) is a diverse community collaborative whose members are trained in mediation techniques to help students and families effectively address continuing attendance problems. Program goals of ACT are to provide a second level of truancy intervention for students and families that continue to have attendance problems post-AIM, and to engage the community in identifying and addressing the issues that impact student attendance on a case-by-case basis as well as at the school and community level. Conflict Solution's AIM and ACT have been identified as promising practices (Reimer & Dimock, 2005).

Conflict Solutions served as a neutral facilitator of the community process, a consultant on the use of mediation in truancy intervention, program design and implementation, and assisted with the evaluation design. Conflict Solutions assisted in bringing agencies together, pooling resources, and holding each accountable. In addition to BCSD staff and Conflict Solutions, community partners identified were representatives of the Department of Juvenile Justice (DJJ), Department of Social Services (DSS), Solicitor's Office, DOE/DHEC's State Consultant for School Social Work (working within a partnership between education and health), Department of Mental Health (DMH), various community nonprofits providing services to students, and the three law enforcement agencies sharing jurisdiction within the school district: Berkeley County Sheriff's Department, Moncks Corner Police Department, and the Goose Creek Police Department.

These agencies identified truancy and a slow family court process as frustrations they were all dealing with in their everyday work. They also recognized that as individual agencies they were only one part of the solution and would be much more effective by committing to a common goal and bringing their different areas of expertise and jurisdiction to work collaboratively toward developing an effective community response to truancy.

Reimer and Dimock's (2005) strategy precautions for establishing effective collaboration, guided the process:

1. Leadership must be persistent since only time, and trial and error will bring the right people to the table. Some representatives, present at the early meetings, decided by default not to be regular contributing members of the group. This was still viewed as a success. Just by way of being involved in the initial meetings, knowledge was gained and relationships built for future working together.
2. Disputes over territory must be early and often resolved. The initial meeting of the group, in early summer 2006, was tense

and awkward. Old hurts and faultfinding behaviors were hard to replace. However, it was over the course of the next two meetings that attitudes began to change. Trust developed quickly because of the determination of group members to focus on solutions to truancy.

3. Shared values and desired outcomes will bring cohesiveness to the group and synergy for a combined vision. The final group consisted of those wholly committed to the goal of reducing truancy in the community and who have continued their dedication to the process. Each agency that remained around the table looked at how the family court impasse affected the work they needed to do and how they could contribute to resolving it.

4. Each participant was asked to contribute to the process with their knowledge or their resources. In most instances, the contribution proved to be both knowledge and resources, usually in-kind or by the contribution of personnel.

A helpful survey tool developed by the OMNI Institute for evaluating the effectiveness of community collaboratives and used by the Colorado Foundation for Families and Children in the evaluation of Truancy Reduction Demonstration Programs can be found at: http://www.omni.org/omni_institute.aspx.

The community team, working closely with the social workers, designed a system for early truancy intervention that included a clearly defined process for each of the following phases: (a) Identifying truant students, (b) Assessment, (c) Treatment planning, and (d) Case resolution. These were all steps that are clearly within the job responsibility of the school social workers and their school partners. School social workers identified, via attendance reports, students considered truant and set up meetings with the students and their parents to develop an intervention/treatment plan (AIP). School social workers made home or workplace visits when parents/guardians were unable to come to the school during regular hours. They also performed quality assurance checks on system coding and documentation by the attendance officers.

Many students resolved their attendance issues through the early social work interventions identified in the AIP process; however, there were still some who continued to miss additional days. School social work involvement in the early part of the pilot revealed this problem in the system. They presented two related problems to the team for resolution: What should happen if the truant behavior continues, and what responsibilities do they have at that point?

At this point disparate parts, the agency representatives, school personnel, and social workers truly became a proactive team. The team collaborated to design a secondary intervention process for habitual truants. They became the Attendance Conciliation Team (ACT), previously described, and developed a process for intervention at the next level:

1. Students and parents who did not attend AIP meetings, or violated the AIP agreement, and accumulated two more unlawful absences were referred to ACT and the Solicitor's Office.
2. Once or twice a month, depending on numbers of truants, ACT interventions were scheduled at the district office, where the whole team met with these students and their families. The family was mailed a certified letter and a letter was also hand delivered by an officer from the Berkeley County Sheriff's Department to the home address inviting them to the meeting. This visit by law enforcement, frequently the student's school resource officer (SRO), had a very positive effect on the attendance rate of students and their families at the ACT meetings.
3. The Solicitor's Office started the ACT meetings by explaining the attendance law and the repercussions for violating it, and explained legal rights to the family. Families were then served a summons to appear in court by a Berkeley County deputy.
4. Once a family was served a summons to appear in court, ACT members mediated with individual families and the school social worker to identify issues impacting attendance and collaboratively develop solutions. Recommendations from these agreements were then made to the court (i.e., mental health counseling, medication, parenting classes, etc.).

It was imperative that intervention efforts were not focused on the student alone. This ensured that a holistic approach was applied to each student's case. Efforts that strengthen a family will sustain the efforts of the school social worker and student support team. Mediation, like good social work practice, is most effective when strengths-based and student/family focused. School factors such as positive relationships with teachers, a safe environment, flexibility in meeting students' diverse learning styles, promptly notifying parents about each absence, and consistently and uniformly applying attendance policies contribute to student attendance and decrease the likelihood of truancy (U.S. Department of Education, 2009). Another important school factor that can help students and their families feel connected to school is a welcoming school environment that acknowledges and values the cultures of the diverse student body (Fredricks, Blumenfeld, & Paris, 2004). Additionally, "policies, rules, curriculum, and teacher characteristics can contribute to truancy" (Harding, & Burley, 1998, p. 2).

As described, the Berkeley County School District pilot, following a comprehensive approach, had two perspectives going on at the same time: a student perspective and a systems perspective. The student perspective required individual assessment, treatment, and follow-up; the systems perspective included additional school personnel and community partners and required program assessment and program/policy development. Mediation is a highly effective process that allows individual families to discuss and collaboratively address issues affecting their child's attendance through the aid of a trained neutral third party. Mediation also aids in the identification of systemic issues. Trained volunteer mediators reported to the district and/or program coordinator when there were particular issues that continually resurface over the course of several mediations, indicating a systemic problem. Mediation agreements were also helpful in this manner because they listed the issues and the collaborative solutions developed by the family and school.

Sample Forms

See Appendix A for the following sample forms: Berkeley County School District Attendance Policy; Parent's Notification of Attendance Policy and Laws; Procedure to Process Truancy Cases; Letter of Invitation to Parents to Attend Attendance Intervention Plan Meeting (AIP); Student Attendance Intervention Plan; ACT Mediation Consent Form; Conflict Solutions District Staff Training Manual. (See forms in Appendixes)

Outcomes

The purpose of evaluation is not to find fault, but rather to identify program improvement and to document program effectiveness. The outcome evaluation looks at two levels of data. Overall, district data results were very important for identifying truancy trends across the two schools as the pilot progressed. The district data showed an increase in the percentage of students who were coded correctly as truant into the SASI electronic data system. That increase might lead the casual observer to consider the pilot a failure, but it is only by thoroughly identifying (coding) truant students, by first finding them, that social workers could intervene with students into truancy issues identified.

The school level data also showed a positive reduction in the numbers of truancies while school social workers were employed and can be seen in Figure 7.1 below, with a baseline beginning in 2005–06, the year prior to pilot implementation, showing decrease in truant behavior in 2006–07, and becoming even more successful in the 2007–08 school year. Data for 2008–09 reflects the unfortunate circumstance of the elimination of the school social workers at Sedgefield Middle School and the reduction of the time of the social worker at Berkeley Middle School due to the end of the grant funding and the beginning of national/state cuts to education funding as a result of the economy. It also provides documentation of program success that can be used for future program growth when the school district budgets improve.

Student specific evaluation on the effectiveness of social work intervention is in progress. Many variable points of intervention have been collected about a large number of students and are being analyzed to determine to what extent school social work prevention efforts and individual/group interventions did, in fact, improve the identified student's attendance, behavior in school, grades, and access to medical care, and whether the program helped to reduce the dropout rate. Those results will be completed at a later date. Berkeley County Attendance Date Report in the South Carolina Database.

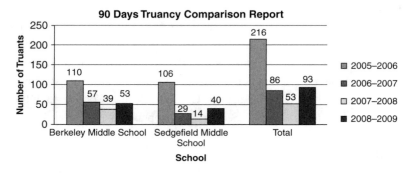

FIGURE 7.1. 90 Days Truancy Comparison Report.

Lessons Learned

Several lessons have been learned through the process of implementing the truancy prevention program in South Carolina. Some of the most important lessons are as follows:

1. District satisfaction with the results of school social work prevention/intervention in the area of student attendance resulted in a BCSD request to the School Board for funding of another school social work position. The request was approved and an additional social worker was hired the following year.
2. Although the development of the community collaborative was a very difficult first step, it developed into a major strength of the pilot.
3. Buy-in for a new process can be slow; yet can be facilitated by including all stakeholders and giving them the positive feedback of outcome improvements. Everyone involved needs to know their contribution is significant.
4. Annual training contributed to an increase in successful coding for truancy documentation. Each year additional staff attended. Annual training kept a focus on the importance of truancy intervention, and fostered networking and positive morale among staff.
5. School social workers can be positive change agents when participating in a school district system design for truancy prevention and intervention.
6. School social workers can have positive impact on an individual student's school attendance behavior.

Success Story

Putting a face on students who have overcome real struggles with attendance problems and are now finding success in school is the most personal way to look at the effectiveness of school social work intervention in truancy. The following case example presents the story of one school social worker that worked with a student of a family who had recently moved to the United States.

The middle school student was experiencing not only the usual transition issues of young adolescents, but also those brought by sudden immersion

---

into a strange culture and a learning environment that required a new language. Although the family was making positive adjustments such as securing employment, buying a home, and working toward citizenship, it was not without struggles. The student initially tried hard to fit in, learn English, and keep up with studies, but it was not long before grades and peer relationships began to suffer. The student became involved with a peer group that was not a good influence and struggled with her parents over the differences in cultural norms. The student began to miss more and more days of school and resisted offers of assistance from concerned teachers. The student's discipline record and grades worsened.

Meeting with the student and her parents to develop an Attendance Improvement Plan, the school social worker learned that the parents had been using the student for translating during important appointments and legal proceedings, thus causing the student to miss school and did not understand how quickly the days added up. A mentor was secured for help with homework and positive role modeling, and grades and behavior at school improved, but struggles at home continued to the point that the student considered running away, among other things. Another meeting was held for the student and family with the school social worker and other student support staff and additional referrals and resources were provided to the family.

A plan was made to "triple team" the student with the mentor, school guidance counselor, and social worker acting as a support team. However, several additional absences required that, according to pilot policy, the student be referred to the ACT for intervention at the second level. Even though the process was clearly explained to the student, it appeared to be very frightening. At the ACT, the student was placed under an Order to Attend, and met with the student support staff to develop an additional action plan. This was the point at which the social worker began to see changes in the student's planning and goal setting. The plan was for the student to attend summer school to help with course work and to attend a high school away from current influences. She hoped to become involved in extracurricular activities. The mentor planned to stay with the student through the first year of high school transition. Through social work counseling sessions, the student developed a clear understanding of how attendance impacts grades and relationships with teachers and peers. While the "red flag" was truancy, as is usually the case, there were many other variables in this student's life. Because of the truancy intervention, this student now has a bright future with support systems in place that will help to impact not only the next few years, but ultimately a lifetime!

Conclusion

This chapter examined a grant funded truancy reduction pilot project that involved using school social work services as an important part of truancy interventions. It discussed experiences with the process of community collaboration, program design and evaluation, as well as the use of school social workers for both program design and direct intervention.

At the district and school level, reduction in the number of students truant, increase in accurate coding, development of a sustainable community collaborative, school-wide system buy-in and participation, as well as the hiring of an additional social worker for the school district were seen as indicators of the pilot's success. Evaluation is ongoing at the individual intervention level. Data has been collected on coding accuracy, timeliness, and specifics of intervention on a large number of cases and will be analyzed to further determine success of the pilot in improved behavior in school, improved grades, access to medical care, and whether the program helped to reduce the dropout rate. These results will be completed at a later date.

Lessons learned throughout the process continued to provide insight for program improvement. These included development of a community-wide collaborative with an agenda focused on truancy issues, which was critical but not easily accomplished, all stakeholders need positive reinforcement, annual training provides not only content, but helps to sustain the system as designed. In addition to the positive impact that school social workers had on individual students' school attendance behavior, they contributed as positive change agents in the district-wide system design, evaluation, and sustainability. A student success story highlighted the difference a school social worker can make for truant students.

Appendixes

Administrative Rule

SCHOOL ATTENDANCE

Code **JBD-R** Issued 06/05

Truancy

Definitions

- **Truant**

  A child ages 6 to 17 meets the definition of a truant when the child has three consecutive unlawful absences or a total of five unlawful absences.

- **Habitual Truant**

  A "habitual" truant is a child, ages 12 to 17 years, who fails to comply with the intervention plan developed by the school, the child, and the parent(s) or guardian(s) and who accumulates two or more additional unlawful absences.

- **Chronic Truant**

  A "chronic" truant is a child, ages 12 to 17 years, who has been through the school intervention process, has reached the level of a "habitual" truant, has been referred to Family Court and placed on an order to attend school, and continues to accumulate unlawful absences.

- **Intervention Plans**

  Each school is responsible for sending the names of the designated person to lead the intervention team to the district office. Once a student is determined to be truant, or after three consecutive unlawful absences or a total of five unlawful absences occur, the attendance officer will attempt to identify the reasons for the student's continued absence and develop a plan in conjunction with the student and parent/guardian to improve future attendance. The attendance officer will develop a written intervention plan.

The plan for improving student attendance will include, but not be limited to, the following:

- designation of a person to lead the intervention team
- reasons for the unlawful absences
- actions to be taken by the parent/guardian and student to resolve the cause of unlawful absences
- documentation of referrals to appropriate service providers and, if applicable, alternative school and community-based providers
- actions to be taken by intervention team members
- actions to be taken in the event unlawful absences continue
- signature of parent/guardian or evidence that attempts were made to involve parent/guardian
- documentation of involvement of team members
- guidelines for making revisions to the plan

■ Referrals and Judicial Intervention

A student ages 6 to 17 years will not be referred to the Family Court to be placed on an order to attend school prior to the written intervention planning being completed with the parent(s) or guardian(s) by the school. Should the parent(s) or guardian(s) refuse to cooperate with the intervention plan to remedy the attendance problem, the District may refer the student to Family or Magistrate Court in accordance with S.C. Code Ann. § 59-65-50 (1990), and file a report against the parent(s) or guardian(s) with the Department of Social Services in compliance with S.C. Code Ann. § 20-7-490(2)(c) (Supp. 2002).

1. Petition for a School Attendance Order

If the intervention plan is not successful and further inquiry by school officials fails to cause the truant student and/or parent(s) or guardian(s) to comply with the written intervention plan, or if the student and/or parent(s) or guardian(s) refuses to participate in intervention and the student accumulates two or more additional unlawful absences, the student will be considered an "habitual" truant. Thereafter, the school attendance officer may refer the student to Family or Magistrate Court for truancy. Each referral must include a copy of the plan and specify any corrective action regarding the student and/or the parent(s) or guardian(s) that the District recommends that the court adopt, as well as any other available programs or alternatives identified by the District. The intervention plan must be attached to the petition to the Family or Magistrate Court and served on the student and the parent(s) or guardian(s).

2. **Petition for Contempt of Court**

   Once a school attendance order has been issued by the Family Court and the student continues to accumulate unlawful absences, the student will be considered to be a "chronic" truant and the District may refer the case back to Family Court. The school and District must exhaust all reasonable alternatives prior to petitioning the Family Court to hold the student and/ or the parent(s) or guardian(s) in contempt of court. Any petition for contempt of court must include a written report indicating the corrective actions that were attempted by the District and what graduated sanctions or alternatives to incarceration are available to the court in the community. The District must include in the written report its recommendation to the court should the student and/or parent(s) or guardian(s) be found in contempt of court.

3. **Inter-Agency Cooperation**

   The District will coordinate with the local office of the Department of Juvenile Justice to establish a system of graduated sanctions and alternatives to incarceration in truancy cases.

Transfer of Plans

If a student transfers to another public school in South Carolina, his/her intervention plan must be forwarded to the receiving school. School officials will contact the parent(s) or guardian(s) and local team members to review the plan and revise as appropriate. Court ordered plans may be amended through application to the court.

Adopted 06/14/05

Process 1

Attendance Policy and Laws

- Students in grades K-8 that accumulate more than ten absences face the possibility of being retained. Students in grades 9-12 that accumulate more than five absences in a semester class or ten days in a year long class face the possibility of losing credit.
- When your child is absent, you must turn in a medical note or parent note within **three** days of their return to school.
- A parent note will excuse a maximum often days in grades K-8. In grades 9–12, a parent note will excuse a maximum of five days in a semester class or ten days in a year long class. *These notes will only be accepted if the absences are considered to be lawful.*
- If notes are not handed in within the 3 day time frame, your child's absences are considered unlawful.
- There are serious consequences for unlawful absences.

Lawful Absences

- Absences that are excused by a doctor or other medical professional
- Death in the immediate family (parent, grandparent, or sibling)
- A recognized religious holiday
- Special circumstances **approved in advance by** the principal. ***You must get approval from an administrator.*** (*Teachers do not have the authority to approve absences for special circumstances*).
- If your child has an illness that will cause him/her to be absent in excess of five days, you must call the school to determine if homebound instruction is appropriate. You must have medical documentation verifying the need for homebound.
- A parent note for illnesses may excuse up to ten days in grades K-8. In grades 9–12, a parent note for illnesses may excuse up to five days in a semester class or 10 days in a year long class.

Unlawful Absences

- An unlawful absence is any absence that is not excused under the conditions mentioned above.

Consequences

- A total of three consecutive or five total unlawful absences is considered to be truancy.
- **Five** unlawful absences will result in a referral to Truancy Mediation/Intervention meeting.
- Refusal to attend truancy mediation/intervention meeting and accumulating two or more unlawful absences after the scheduled mediation/intervention meeting date will result in a referral to family court.
- Parents convicted for educational neglect may be placed under court order, fined up to $50 a day, and/or imprisoned for up to thirty days in jail for each unexcused absence thereafter.
- Students between the ages of twelve and seventeen years of age may be prosecuted for truancy in family court. This could result in the child being placed in a DJJ facility for a period of 30 to 90 days and will result in the child having a criminal record.

A Court Order may remain in effect until a child reaches 17 years of age or completes high school.
Berkeley County School District

Please sign and return by the 1ˢᵗ day of school:_____

Procedure to Process Truancy Cases

Attendance Intervention Plan (AIP)

1. Must be **original** AIP form.
2. Signatures must be in **blue ink.**
3. Must contain the minor, minor's parent/guardian/custodian, and attendance clerk's or school designee's signature and date of the signature.
4. An AIP is only good for the <u>current school year</u> and these steps will need to be followed each new school year.
5. The student's address must include a current physical address.

Documentation

1. Document dates and names of anyone you speak with by phone or in person.
2. Provide a copy of the dated **Letter of Invitation** for the AIP meeting that was mailed to the parent.
3. If the parent's signature is not on the AIP due to a **'no show':**
   • Document the date on the AIP when the signed/completed AIP was mailed to the parent
   • Provide a copy of the dated **Letter of Invitation** for the AIP meeting that was mailed to the parent (the date in the letter must be the same date the student and school representative has signed the AIP).

AIP for Students withdrawn/dropped

1. As long as an AIP was signed prior to the withdrawal of the student, you can proceed with the Juvenile Petition.
2. If an AIP was not signed prior to the withdrawal of the student: Make every effort to get the student re-enrolled and determine if it is a DSS or DJJ issue (see page 3).
   Once the student is re-enrolled & it is determined to be a DJJ issue, have the student & parent sign the AIP at re-enrollment. If it is a DSS issue, make the referral to DSS, not DJJ.

Juvenile Petition

Juvenile Petitions are only submitted for first time truant students (a minimum of 3 consecutive or 5 total unlawful absences).

1. Must be **original** document
2. Signatures must be in **blue ink**
3. The name of the legal guardian or parent must match the signature of the person signing the AIP.
   It is best to avoid signatures of step parents who are not legal guardians.
   The DSS worker must be notified for foster care children.
4. List **2 full unexcused absences after** the AIP is signed.
   Do not include dates prior to the AIP signatures.
5. Attach the student's attendance record with the petition.
   Dates listed on the AIP must match attendance records of the student that are sent with the petition.
6. If the parent/guardian signed the AIP on a different date than the student and the school designee, then the unexcused dates on the Juvenile Petition must be after the date the parent signed the AIP.

Juvenile Verification

Must be the **original** and include the signatures in **blue ink** of both you and the notary.

Submitting an Affidavit for Contempt of the Consent Order

Affidavits are only submitted if an order to Attend/Consent Order has been signed and filed and student has further violations.

1. Must be the **original** and include the signatures of both you and the notary.
2. Must be in **blue ink.**
3. One more unexcused absence, tardies/cuts, and suspensions (in or out of school) are all violations of the consent order and **all violations** must be included on the affidavit.
4. In paragraph/sentence #3 of the affidavit, it asks for the date the Consent Order was filed, use the filed date on the Consent Order.
5. Look for the "stamp" that says Filed, then it gives the date, then it says Mary P. Brown, Clerk of Court, Berkeley County, SC.

---

6. Attendance and discipline records must be attached and include the dates/violations that are listed on the affidavit.

If the packet is not completed as desribed, the entire packet will be returned to Phyliss Thornthwaite. The school will have ten (10) days to make these corrections and return the packet. **If the corrections are not received within ten (10) days, the case will be Nolle Pross/Dismissed.**

Things to Remember:

All paperwork must be mailed to:
> **Department of Juvenile Justice**
> **103 Gulledge Street**
> **Attn: Barbara McHoney**
> **Moncks Corner, SC 29461**

Once DJJ receives your paperwork, they will process it and forward it to the Solicitor's Office for action.

April 15th is the cut off date to submit a juvenile Petition for truancy (petitions received after this date will not be scheduled or filed).

An **Affidavit for Contempt of Court** can still be submitted until the end of the school year.

If you feel the non-attendance is based on educational neglect (the parent is at fault for not sending the minor to school), this must be referred to the Department of Social Services (DSS), NOT the Department of Juvenile Justice (DJJ). If the referral is made to DSS, you cannot send a referral to DJJ.

> Students under the age of **twelve (12)** that is considered truant should be referred to **DSS.**

DJJ (Department of Juvenile Justice)-handles minors (in Family Court) who have received charges.

DSS (Department of Social Services)-handles adults (in Family Court) who are or may be charged with neglect/abuse.

Letter of Invitation:
Attendance Intervention Plan Meeting

Date: _____

To the Parents of: _____,
Student's Name

Our school attendance records show that your child has had ____ unlawful absences from school this school year. Not only is this a serious loss of your child's education, but the absences are a violation of Berkeley County School District attendance policy and the South Carolina Schools Compulsory Attendance Law.

As required by law, Berkeley County School District must develop an **Attendance Intervention Plan** for your child. It is very important for you to participate in the development of the **Plan**.

A meeting has been scheduled for _____.
Date and Time of Meeting

The meeting will be held at: _____.
School and Location

If you cannot participate in this meeting, an **Attendance Intervention Plan** will be developed and sent to you for your signature. However, if you cannot attend but would like to participate through a telephone conference, please call the school and talk to:

_____

Name and Phone Number of School Contact Person

We look forward to your participation in the development your child's **Attendance Intervention Plan**. We hope that the **Attendance Intervention Plan** will avoid any further legal action required regarding your child and the Compulsory Attendance Law.

Sincerely,

_____

School Documentation

Date of Phone Call to Parent/Guardian to Schedule Meeting: _____
Results of Phone Call: ☐ Parent/Guardian will attend ☐ Parent/Guardian will not attend
    ☐ Parent/Guardian wants meeting rescheduled for (Date and Time): _____
    ☐ Other:_____

Berkeley County Student Attendance Intervention Plan

Conference Date: _____

> *If a student has 2 more unexcused absences following the development of the AIP, a Truancy Referral Packet should be made to the Department of Juvenile Justice.*

Identification Information

Student's Name: _____ DOB: _____

School: _____ ID#: _____

Address: _____

Parent/Legal Guardian: _____

Home Phone: (_____)_____ Cell Phone: (_____)_____

Work Phone: (_____)_____ Emergency Phone: (_____)_____

Attendance Policy given and reviewed _____ **(Date and Initials of parent/guardian) Student Attendance History** (*days absent, past problems, previous schools, etc.*):

_____

_____

_____

_____

_____

Designated Intervention Team Leader: _____

Intervention Planning Participants:

• Parent/Guardian: _____

• Student: _____

• School Representative: _____

• Social Worker: _____

_____

• Counselor: _____

• Attendance clerk: _____

• Other: _____

Questions to be asked by school representative:
(To ask student) What are the reasons you are not coming to school?

_____

_____

(To ask parent) What do you think are the reasons your child is not coming to school?

_____

_____

School representative to ask both family and student: What will help?

_____

_____

Student agrees to: _____

_____

Date to begin: _____

Parent agrees to: _____

Date to begin: _____

School agrees to: _____

Date to begin: _____

I. Collaborative recommendations of the student, parent/guardian, and school personnel to solve the attendance problem:
   ☐ _____

II. Actions to be taken in the event unlawful absences continue:
   ☐ _____

III. Referrals have been made to the following service providers and alternative school and community-based programs: _____

_____

IV. Weekly attendance will be monitored by: _____

Social Worker comments: _____

_____

_____

_____

_____
Plan Approval Date

_____   _____
Student's Signature   Parent/Guardian's Signature

_____   _____
School Official's Signature   Parent/Guardian's Signature

Signatures should be in Blue Ink and dates signed by the parent on the AIP must match the date and time on the Letter of Invitation.

Date copy of AIP was mailed to the parent: _____

Date of telephone conversations: _____

This intervention plan was adapted from a similar document found in the manual entitled "Guidelines for Improved Student Attendance and Truancy Prevention," which was developed by Chicago Public Schools' Office of Instruction and School Management.

ACT

(Attendance Conciliation Team)
Berkeley County School District
229 East Main Street
PO Box 608
Moncks Corner, SC 29461

MEMORANDUM OF AGREEMENT

Date of Mediation: _____ Number of Unlawful Absences: _____

Name of Parties (print): _____

Issues Affecting Attendance:

We Agree to the Following:

The attendance policy and repercussions for noncompliance have been explained to the family.

We have mediated the issues regarding attendance and we intend to follow this resolution in good faith.

Parties Signature: _____   _____

_____   _____

References

Achievement for Latinos through Academic Success (ALAS). Retrieved on June 20, 2009, from http://www.ndpc-sd.org/dissemination/model_programs.php

Adams, M., Bell, L., & Griffin, P. (2004). *Teaching for diversity and social justice.* New York, NY: Routledge.

Alberts, M. (2009, Summer). *Poverty and children's learning.* Consortium Connection. Minneapolis, MN: University of Minnesota.

Allen-Meares, P., Washington, R., & Welsh, B. (2000). *Social work services in schools* (3rd ed.). Boston, MA: Allyn and Bacon.

Allensworth, E., & Easton, J. (2007). *What matters for staying on-track and graduating in Chicago Public High Schools: A close look at course grades, failures and attendance in the freshman year.* Chicago: Consortium on Chicago School Research.

Attwood, G. & Croll, P. (2006). Truancy in secondary school pupils: Prevalence, trajectories and pupil perspectives. *Research Papers in Education, 21*(4), 467–484.

Baker, J., Derrer, R., Davis, S., Dinklage-Travis, H., Linder, D., & Nicholson, M. (2001). The flip side of the coin: Understanding the school's contribution to dropout and completion. *School Psychology Quarterly, 16*(4), 406–426.

Baker, M.L., Sigmon, J.N., & Nugent, M.E. (2001). *Truancy reduction: Keeping students in school.* Bulletin. Washington, DC. U.S. Department of Justice, Office of Justice Programs, Office of Juvenile Justice and Delinquency Prevention. Retrieved January 13, 2009, from http://www.ncjrs.gv/html/ojjdp/jjbul2001_9_1/contents.html

Banks, J. (2004). Multicultural education: Historical development, dimensions and practice. In J. A. Banks & C. A. Banks (Eds.), *Handbook of research on multicultural education* (2nd ed., pp. 3–29), San Francisco: Jossey Bass.

Batsche, G., Elliott, J., Graden, J. L., Grimes, J., Kovaleski, J. F., Prasse, D., et al. (1994). Truancy intervention. *Journal of Research and Development in Education, 27,* 203–211.

Belfanz, R., Herzog, L., & Mac Iver, D. (2007). Preventing student disengagement and keeping students on the graduation path in urban middle-grades schools: Early identification and effective interventions. *Educational psychologist, 42*(4), 223–225.

Braaksma Fynaardt, A. & Richardson, J. (in press). Tier 2 targeted group interventions. In J. Clark & M. Alvarez (in press), *Response to intervention: A guide for school social workers* (chap. 6). New York: Oxford University Press.

Braithwaite K. S., & James, C. E. (1996). *Educating African Canadians.* Toronto: James Lorimer & Company Ltd.

Bushnell, B., & Card, K. (2003). *Report on longitudinal effects of the WhyTry Program at Pleasant Grove High School* [unpublished]. Retrieved November 1, 2008, from http://www.whytry.org/research.php

Capps, W. R. (2003). The new face of truancy. *School Administration, 60*(4), 34.

Center for the Study of Prevention and Violence (2009). Retrieved May 30, 2009, from www.colorado.edu/cspv/blueprints/matrixfiles/criteria.pdf

Chang, H., & Romero, M. (2008). *Present, engaged, and accounted for: The critical importance of addressing chronic absence in the early grades.* New York: NY: National Center for Children in Poverty, Columbia University.

Children's Law Office. (2006). *Truancy guide: A training and resource manual for truancy intervention.* Columbia, SC: University of South Carolina School of Law.

Clark, J., & Tilly, W. D. (in press). The evolution of response to intervention. In J. Clark & M. Alvarez (in press), *Response to intervention: A guide for school social workers* (chap. 1). New York: Oxford University Press.

Colasanti, M. (2007). *Sanctions on driving privileges.* Denver, CO: Education Commission of the States. Retrieved August 18, 2009, from http://www.ecs.org/clearinghouse/60/10/6010.pdf

Curtis, B., Livingstone, D. W., & Smaller, H. (1992). *Stacking the deck: The streaming of working-class kids in Ontario schools.* Toronto: Our Schools/Our Selves Education Foundation.

David, J. (2008). Poverty and learning: Teacher recruitment incentives. *Educational Leadership, 56*(7), 84–86.

Davies, J. D., & Lee, J. (2006). To attend or not to attend? Why some students choose school and others reject it. *Support for Learning, 21*(4), 204–209.

Deford, Susan. (2007, October 25). Law punishes truancy by taking away teen's keys. *The Washington Post,* pp. AA07. Retrieved February 20, 2009, from http://www.washingtonpost.com/wp-dyn/content/article/2007/10/24/AR2007102400785.html

Delpit, L. (1995). *Other people's children: Cultural conflict in the classroom.* New York, NY: The New Press.

DeSocio, J., VanCura, M., Nelson, L. A., Hewitt, G., Kitzman, H., & Cole, R. (2007). Engaging truant adolescents: Results from a multifaceted intervention pilot. *Preventing School Failure, 51*(3), 3–11.

Dei, G. (1996). *Anti-racism education: Theory and practice.* Halifax, Nova Scotia: Fernwood Publishing.

Duarte, R., & Escario, J. (2006). Alcohol abuse and truancy among Spanish adolescents: A count-data approach. *Economic of Education Review, 25*(2), 179–187.

Dube, S. R., & Orpinas, P. (2009). Understanding excessive school absenteeism as school refusal behavior. *Children & Schools, 31*(2), 87–95.

Duffy, H. (2007). *Meeting the needs of significantly struggling learners in high school: A look at approaches to tiered intervention.* American Institutes for Research. Retrieved May 21, 2009, from http://www.betterhighschools.org/docs/NHSC_RTIBrief_08-02-07.pdf

Eaton, D. K., Brener, N., & Kann, L. K. (2008). Associations of health risk behaviors with school absenteeism: Does having permission for the absence make a difference? *Journal of School Health, 78*(4), 223–229.

Eggett, G. D. (2003). An intervention to mediate motivational shortcomings caused by childhood maltreatment. Unpublished doctoral dissertation, Nova Southeastern University, Ft. Lauderdale, FL.

Ellingson, S. A., Miltenberger, R. G., Stricker, J., Galensky, T. L., & Garlinghouse, M. (2000). Functional assessment and intervention for challenging behaviors in the classroom by general classroom teachers. *Journal of Positive Behavior Interventions, 2,* 85–97.

Epstein, J. L., & Sheldon, S. B. (2002). Present and accounted for, improving student attendance through family and community involvement. *Journal of Educational Research, 95*(5), 308–318.

Evelo, D., Sinclair, M., Hurley, C., Christenson, S., & Thurlow, M. (1996). *Keeping kids in school: Using check & connect for dropout prevention.* Minneapolis: Institute on Community Integration, University of Minnesota.

Fallis, R. K., & Opotow, S. (2003). Are students failing school or are schools failing students? Class cutting in high school. *Journal of Social Issues, 59,* 103–109.

Fantuzzo, J., Grim, S., & Hazan, H. (2005). Project start: An evaluation of a community-wide school-based intervention to reduce truancy. *Psychology in the Schools, 42*(6), 657–667.

Fleras, (2001). *Social problems in Canada: Condition, construction, and challenges.* Toronto: Prentice Hall.

Fredricks, J., Blumenfeld, P., & Paris, A. (2004). School engagement: Potential of the concept, state of evidence. *Review of Educational Research, 74*(1), 59–109.

Garry, E. M. (1996). *Truancy: First step to a lifetime of problems.* Bulletin. Washington, DC. U.S. Department of Justice, Office of Justice Programs, Office of Juvenile Justice and Delinquency Prevention. Retrieved January 13, 2009, from http://www.ncjrs.gov/pdffiles/truancy.pdf

Gentle-Genitty, C. (2009). Truancy: The need to track more than absences. *Network: Indiana University School of Social Work & Alumni News, Winter,* 8–11.

Harding, E., & Burley, M. (1998). *Truant students: Evaluating the impact of the "Becca Bill" Truancy petition requirements*. Olympia, WA: Washington State Institute for Public Policy.

Hardy, K., & Lazloffy, T. (2007). *Teens who hurt*. New York: Guilford Press.

Harlow, C. W. (2003). *Education and correctional populations*. Bureau of Justice Statistics Special Report, NCJ 195670. Washington, DC: U.S. Department of Justice.

Haynes, J. M. (2005). *The impact of race and class on the educational experiencesof black students in Ottawa's educational system*. Montreal: McGill University Press.

Heibrunn, J. (2003). *The costs and benefits of three intensive interventions with Colorado truants*. Denver: National Center for School Engagement. Retrieved June 11, 2009, from http://www.schoolengagement.org/index.cfm/Our%20Services

Heilbrunn, J. Z. (2006). *Alternatives to juvenile detention: Effective strategies for working with truant youth*. Denver, CO: National Center for School Engagement.

Heilbrunn, J. (2007). *Pieces of the truancy jigsaw: A literature review*. Denver, CO: National Center for School Engagement. Colorado Foundation for Families and Children. Retrieved August 18, 2009, from http://ncjrs.org/pdffiles1/ojjdp/truancy_toolkt_2.pdf

Henry, K. (2007). Who's skipping school: Characteristics of truants in 8th and 10th grade. *Journal of School Health, 77*(1), 29–35.

Henry, K., & Huizinga, D. (2005). *The effect of truancy on the onset of drug use and delinquency*. Paper presented at the National Criminal Justice Association Annual Meeting, Toronto, November 16, 2005.

Heppen, J., & Therriault, S. (2008). *Developing early warning systems to identify potential high school dropouts*. Washington, DC: National High School Center/ American Institutes for Research.

Hopkins, R. (1997). *Educating black males: Critical lessons in schooling, community, and power*. New York: State University of New York Press.

Howe, K. R. (1997). *Understanding equal educational opportunity: Social justice, democracy and schooling*. New York: Teachers College Press.

Hubbard, B. (2005, May 16). A class divided: Examining the chasm between students success, failure. *Rocky Mountain News*.

Huxtable, M. (2007). International school social work. In L. Bye & M. Alvarez (Eds.), *School social work: Theory to practice* (pp. 310–326). Belmont, CA: Thomson Brooks/Cole.

Ingram, K., Lewis-Palmer, T., Sugai, G. (2005). Function-based intervention planning: Comparing the effectiveness of FBA function-based and non-function-based intervention plans. *Journal of Positive Behavior Interventions, 7*,4, 224–236.

Intercultural Development Research Association (IDRA). (2009). *Coca-Cola valued youth program*. Retrieved on June 16, 2009, from http://www.idra.org/Coca-Cola_Valued_Youth_Program.html/

James, D. J. (2004). *Profile of jail inmates, 2002.* Washington DC: Bureau of Justice Statistics, Office of Justice Programs, U.S. Department of Justice.

James. C. (1998). Up to no good: Black on the streets and encountering police. In V. Satzewich (Ed.), *Racism & social inequality in Canada* (pp. 157–178). Toronto: Thompson Educational Publishing.

Joseph, Mary Ann, (2006). *Truancy: Prevention and intervention: School resource manual.* Conflict Solutions, LLC, P.O. Box 1318, Georgetown, SC 29442.

Kailin, J. (2004). *Antiracist education: From theory to practice.* New York: Rowman & Littlefield Publishers, Inc.

Kearney, C. A., & Bates, M. (2005). Addressing school refusal behavior: Suggestions for frontline professionals. *Children & Schools, 27*, 4, 107–216.

Kearney, C. A., Lemons, A., & Silverman, J. (2004). The functional assessment of school refusal behavior. *The Behavior Analyst Today, 5*(3), 275–283.

Kearney, C.A. (2007). Forms and functions of school refusal behavior in youth: An empirical analysis of absenteeism severity. *Journal of Child Psychology and Psychiatry, 48*, 53–61

Kim, J. S., & Streeter, C. (2006). Increasing school attendance: Effective strategies and interventions. In C. Franklin, M. B. Harris, & P. Allen-Meares (Eds.), *The school services sourcebook: A guide for school-based professionals.* New York, NY: Oxford University Press.

Kramer, E.M. (2003). *The emerging monoculture: Assimilation and the "model minority."* Westport, CT: Praeger.

Laird, J., DeBell, M., & Chapman, C. (2006). *Dropout rates in the United States.* Washington, DC: National Center for Education Statistics. Retrieved June 10, 2009, from http://nces.ed.gov/pubs2007/2007024.pdf

Lara-Cinisomo, S., Pebley, A., Vaiana, M., Maggio, E., Berends, M., & Luca, S. (2004, Fall). *A matter of class: Educational achievement reflects family background more than ethnicity or immigration.* Rand Review. Obtained August 27, 2009, from http://www.rand.org/publications/randreview/issues/fall2004/class.html

Lehr, C. A., Sinclair, M. F., & Christenson, S. (2004). Addressing student engagement and truancy prevention during the elementary school years: A replication study of the check & connect model. *Journal of Education for Students Placed at Risk, 9*, 279–301.

Levy, H., & Henry, K. (2007). Mistaking attendance. *The New York Times*, September 2.

Lyon, A. R., & Colter, S. (2007). Toward reduced bias and increased utility in the assessment of school refusal behavior: The case for diverse samples and evaluations of context. *Psychology in the Schools, 44*(6), 551–565.

Marsiglia, F. F., & Kulis, S. (2009). *Culturally grounded social work. Diversity, oppression, and change*. Chicago: Lyceum Books, Inc.

Maslow, Abraham H. (1987). *Motivation and personality* (3rd ed.). New York: Longman.

Martin, D. (2007, March 1). Arthur Schlesinger, Historian of Power, Dies at 89. *New York Times*. Retrieved November 29, 2009, from www.nytimes.com/2007/03/01/washington/01schlesinger.html?

McCluskey, C. P., Bynum, T. S., & Patchini, J. W. (2004). Reducing chronic absenteeism: An assessment of an early truancy initiative. *Crime Delinquency, 50*(2), 214–234.

McCray, E. D. (2006). It's 10 a.m.: Do you know where your children are? *Intervention in School and Clinic, 42*(1), 30–33.

McLaren, P. (2000). White terror and oppositional agency: Towards a critical multiculturalism. In E. M. Duarte & S. Smith (2000). *Foundational perspectives in multicultural education*. New York: Longman.

Meyer, K. A. (1999). Functional analysis and treatment of problem behavior exhibited by elementary school children. *Journal of Applied Behavior Analysis, 32*, 229–232.

Mogulescu, S., & Segal, H. (2002). *Approaches to truancy prevention*. Retrieved June 23, 2009, available from http://www.vera.org/content/approaches-truancy-prevention

Mueller, D., Giacomazzi, A., & Stoddard, C. (2006). Dealing with chronic absenteeism and its related consequences: The process and short-term effects of a diversionary juvenile court intervention. *Journal of Education for Students Placed at Risk, 11*(2), 199–219.

Muscott, H. S., Mann, E. L., & LeBrun, M. R. (2008). Positive behavioral interventions and supports in New Hampshire: Effects of large-scale implementation of school-wide positive behavior support on student discipline and academic achievement. *Journal of Positive Behavior Interventions, 10*(3), 190–205.

National Association of School Psychologists (NASP). (2002). *Interventions for academic and behavior problems II: Preventive and remedial approaches* (Chapter 12, "School Environments"; Figure 2, "Continuum of Behavioral Support: Designing School-Wide Systems for Student Success"). Bethesda, MD: National Association of School Psychologists.

National Center for Education Statistics. (2005). *Building a culture of quality data*. Retrieved June 8, 2009, from http://nces.ed.gov/forum/pub_2005801.asp

National Center for Education Statistics. (2007a). National Forum on Education Statistics. Retrieved June 8, 2009, from http://nces.ed.gov/forum/annual_report_0607.asp

National Center for Education Statistics. (2007b). Summer 2007 meeting recap: Attendance working group. *The Forum Voice, 10*(2). Retrieved May 21, 2009, from http://nces.ed.gov/forum/v_fall_07.asp

National Center for Education Statistics. (2009a). Chapter 1: Background. *Every school day counts: The Forum guide to collecting and using attendance data.* Retrieved June 8, 2009, from http://nces.ed.gov/pubs2009/attendancedata/chapter1b.asp

National Center for Education Statistics. (2009b). *Public school graduates and dropouts from the common core of data: School year 2006–07.* Retrieved November 29, 2009, from http://nces.ed.gov/pubsearch/pubsinfo.asp?pubid=2010313

National Center for Education Statistics. (2009c). Chapter 2: Attendance codes taxonomy category descriptions. *Every school day counts: The Forum guide to collecting and using attendance data.* Retrieved June 8, 2009, from http://nces.ed.gov/pubs2009/attendancedata/chapter2a.asp

National Center for Education Statistics. (2009d). Chapter 3: Common challenges to collecting attendance code data and effective practices. *Every school day counts: The Forum guide to collecting and using attendance data.* Retrieved June 8, 2009, from http://nces.ed.gov/pubs2009/attendancedata/chapter3a.asp

National Center for Educational Statistics. (2009e). *Condition of education 2009.* Retrieved November 29, 2009, from http://nces.ed.gov/pubsearch/pubsinfo.asp?pubid=2009081

National Center for Education Statistics (2009f). Chapter 4: Data Preparation. *School survey on crime and safety 2005.* Retrieved August 27, 2009, from http://nces.ed.gov/surveys/ssocs/tables/scs_2005_tab_19.asp

National Center for Mental Health Promotion and Youth Violence Prevention (2007, March). *Prevention brief.* Retrieved June 11, 2009, from http://promoteprevent.org/Publications/enewsletters/2007/march07.html

National Center for School Engagement (NCSE). (2005). *The legal and economic implications for truancy executive summary.* Denver, CO: Author. Retrieved June 11, 2009, from http://ojjdp.ncjrs.gov/publications/truancy_toolkit.html

National Center for School Engagement. (2006a). *Guidelines for a national definition of truancy and calculating rates.* Denver, CO: Author. Retrieved June 11, 2009, from http://www.schoolengagement.org/TruancypreventionRegistry/Admin/Resources/Resources/GuidelinesforaNationalDefinitionofTruancyand CalculatingRates.pdf

National Center for School Engagement. (2006b). *Assessing the prevalence of truancy: A four piece puzzle.* Denver, CO: Author. Retrieved June 11, 2009, from http://www.schoolengagement.org/TruancypreventionRegistry/Admin/Resources/Resources/AssessingthePrevalenceofTruancyAFourPiecePuzzle.pdf

National Center for School Engagement. (2006c). *School policies that engage students and families*. Denver, CO: Colorado Foundation for Families and Children. Retrieved August 27, 2009 from http://74.125.95.132/search? q=cache:Hl7-EzpXM7kJ:www.schoolengagement.org/TruancypreventionReg istry/Admin/Resources/Resources/SchoolPoliciesthatEngageStudentsand Families.pdf

National Center for School Engagement. (2007). *The Truancy Reduction Application Interface*. Retrieved November 29, 2009, from http://www.school engagement.org/index.cfm/TRAIN

National Center for School Engagement. (2009a). *Factors contributing to truancy*. Denver, CO: Colorado Foundation for Families and Children. Retrieved August 27, 2009, from http://www.schoolengagement.org/TruancypreventionRegistry/ Admin/Resources/Resources/40.pdf

National Center for School Engagement. (2009b). *The NCSE approach*. Retrieved June 6, 2009, from http://www.schoolengagement.org/index.cfm/NCSE%20Approach

National Center for School Engagement. (2009c). *School policies that engage students and families*. Denver, CO: Colorado Foundation for Families and Children. Retrieved August 30, 2009, from http://www.schoolengagement. org/TruancypreventionRegistry/Admin/Resources/Resources/SchoolPolicies thatEngageStudentsandFamilies.pdf

National Center on Secondary Education and Transition (NSET). (2009). *Part III: What works in dropout prevention? Sample dropout intervention program achieve- ment for Latinos through academic success (ALAS)*. Retrieved on June 20, 2009, from http://www.ncset.org/publications/essentialtools/dropout/part3.3.01.asp

National Dropout Prevention Center (NDPC). (2009). *Big ideas: National dropout prevention strategies*. Retrieved on June 20, 2009 from http://www.dropout prevention.org/model_programs/default.htm.

National Dropout Prevention Center Network. (2009). *Model programs*. Retrieved June 5, 2009, from http://ndpc-web.clemson.edu/modelprograms/rating_ system.php

National Forum on Education Statistics. (2006). *Accounting for every student: A taxonomy for standard student exit codes* (NFES 2006-804.). Department of Education. Washington, DC: National Center for Education Statistics.

National Governors' Association. (2004, August 3). *Recruiting high quality teachers, and keeping them states employ different strategies to keep schools stocked with best and brightest teachers*. Retrieved August 27, 2009 http://www.nga.org/

National Register of Evidence-based Programs and Practices. (2007a). Lions Quest Skills for Adolescence. Washington, DC: SAMHSA. Retrieved November 30, 2009 from http://www.nrepp.samhsa.gov/programfulldetails. asp?PROGRAM_ID=99#outcomes

National Register of Evidence-based Programs and Practices. (2007b). Early Risers Skills for Success. Washington, DC: SAMHSA. Retrieved November 30, 2009 from http://www.nrepp.samhsa.gov/programfulldetails.asp?PROGRAM_ID=128

National Research Council Committee on Increasing High School Students' Engagement and Motivation to Learn. (2004). *Engaging schools: Fostering high school students' motivation to learn.* Washington, DC: The National Academies Press.

Nieto, S. (2004). Affirming diversity: The sociopolitical context of multicultural education. In J. Banks & C. McGee Banks (2004), *Multicultural education: Issues and perspectives.* New Jersey: John Wiley & Sons.

Nieto, S. (2000) *Affirming diversity: The sociopolitical context of multicultural education.* New York, NY: Longman.

Oakes, J. (1985). *Keeping track: How schools structure inequality.* New Haven, CT: Yale University Press.

Office of Juvenile Justice and Delinquency Prevention (OJJDP). (2009). *Model programs.* Retrieved June 1, 2009, from http://www.dsgonline.com/mpg2.5/ratings.htm

Olson, B. (2008). The case for inclusion of sexual orientation and gender identity/expression in school district harassment and violence policies. *National Association of Social Workers, School Social Work Section Connection, 2,* 3–7.

Orfield, G. (2003). *Common core of data local educational agency and school surveys.* Washington, DC: National Center for Education Statistics.

Orfield, G. (2004). *Dropouts in America: Confronting the graduation rate crisis.* Cambridge, MA: Harvard Education Press.

Osterman, K. (2000, Fall). Students' need for belonging in the school community. *Review of Educational Research, 70*(3), 323–367.

Pellerin, L. (2000). *Urban youth and schooling: The effect of school climate on student disengagement and dropout.* Paper presented at the Annual Meeting of the American Educational Research Association (New Orleans, LA, April 24–28, 2000). Additional funding provided by the Royster Society of Fellows. ERIC Docment ED441883.

PEW Charitable Trust. (2008). *One in 100: Behind bars in America.* Retrieved May 25, 2009, from http://www.pewtrusts.org/our_work_report_detail.aspx?id=35900&category=356&WT.srch&source=google

Planty, M., Hussar, W., Snyder, T., Kena, G., KewalRamani, A., Kemp, J., et al., (2009). *The condition of education 2009.* Washington, DC: U.S. Department of Education and the National Center for Educational Statistics. Retrieved May 25, 2009, from http://nces.ed.gov/programs/coe/2009/pdf/28_2009.pdf.

Promising Practices Network (PPN). (2009). *Programs that work: Achievement for Latinos through academic success.* Retrieved on June 20, 2009, from http://www.promisingpractices.net/program.asp?programid=158#programinfo.

Raines, J. (in press). Evidence-based school social work practice & RtI. In J. Clark & M. Alvarez (Eds.), *Response to intervention: A guide for school social workers* (chap. 13). New York: Oxford University Press.

Raines, J. C., & Alvarez, M. (2006). Cash through collaboration: A relational approach to grant writing for social workers in schools. *Children in Schools, 30* (2), 45–63.

Reid, K. (2003). A strategic approach to tackling school absenteeism and truancy: The PSCC scheme. *Educational Studies, 29,* 4, 351–371.

Reimer, M., & Dimock, K. (2005). *Truancy prevention in action: Best practices and model truancy programs.* Clemson, SC: National Dropout Prevention Center/Network, Clemson University.

Repp, A. C., Felce, D., & Barton, L. E. (1998). Basing the treatment of stereotypic and self-injurious behaviors on hypotheses of their causes. *Journal of Applied Behavior Analysis, 21*(3), 281–289.

Reyhner, J. (1991). *Plans for dropout prevention and special school support services for American Indian and Alaska Native Students.* Washington, DC: Department of Education, Indian Nations at Risk Task Force.

Sailor, W., Zuna, N., Jeong-Hoon, C., Thomas, J., McCart, A., & Roger, B. (2006). Anchoring school-wide positive behavior support in structural school reform. *Research & Practice for Persons with Severe Disabilities, 31*(1), 18–30.

SAMHSA. National Registry of Evidenced-Based Programs and Practices. (2009). Retrieved May 1, 2009, from http://www.nrepp.samhsa.gov/

School-wide Information System (SWIS). (2009). *Overview of SWIS.* Retrieved June 15, 2009, from http://www.swis.org/index.php?page=getSWIS Overview

Schrag, J., & Tilly, W. D. (2005). *Response to intervention: Policy considerations and implementation.* Alexandria, VA: National Association of State Directors of Special Education.

Seeley, K. (2006). Guidelines for national definition of truancy and calculating rates. Denver, CO: National Center for School Engagement. Retrieved February 2, 2009, from http://www.schoolengagement.org/TruancypreventionRegistry/Admin/Resources/Resources/GuidelinesforaNationalDefinitionofTruancyand CalculatingRates.pdf

Shaffer, G. (2007). History of school social work. In L. Bye & M. Alvarez (Eds.), *School social work: Theory to practice* (pp. 2–20). Belmont, CA: Brooks/Cole/Thompson/Wadsworth.

Slavin, R. E. (2004). Built to last. *Remedial and Special Education, 25*(1), 61–66.

Smink, J., & Heilbrunn, J. (2005). *Truancy prevention in action: Legal and economic implications of truancy*. Clemson, SC: National Dropout Prevention Center/ Network.

Smink, J., & Reimer, M. (2005). *Fifteen effective strategies for improving student attendance and truancy prevention*. Clemson, SC: National Dropout Prevention Center.

Soldz, S., Huuyser, D., & Dorsey, E. (2003). The cigar as a drug delivery device: Youth use of blunts. *Addiction, 98*, 1379–1386.

Solomon, R. P. (1992). *Black resistance in high school: Forging a separatist culture*. Albany: State University of New York Press.

Spaulding, S. A., Horner, R. H., May, S. L., & Vincent, C. G. (2008). *Implementation of SWPBS across the United States*. Retrieved May 31, 2009, from http://www.pbis.org/evaluation/evaluation_briefs/nov_08_(2).aspx

Stillwell, R. (2009). *Public school graduates and dropouts from the Common Core Data: School year 2006–2007*. Washington, DC: National Center for Education Statistics.

Teasley, M. L. (2004). Absenteeism and truancy: Risk, protection, and best practice implications for school social workers. *Children & Schools, 26*(2), 117–128.

Tierney, W. G. (1993). The college experience of Native Americans: A critical analysis. In L. Weis & M. Fine (Eds.), *Beyond silenced voices: Understanding equal educational opportunity; Social justice, democracy, and schooling* (pp. 309–324). New York: Teachers College Press.

Tischelle, G. (2002, April 4). Battling truancy with wireless devices: Wireless technology may make it harder for students in Boston to play hooky. *Information Week*. Retrieved August 25, 2009, from http://www.information-week.com/news/software/showArticle.jhtml?articleID=6502180

U.S. Department of Education. (2004). *Safe and Drug-Free Schools Communities Act*. Retrieved August 19, 2009, from http://www.ed.gov/programs/dvpformula/ guidance.doc

U.S. Department of Education. (2008). *Truancy: A serious problem for students, schools, and society*. Retrieved February 2, 2009, from http://www.ed.gov/ admins/lead/safety/training/truancy/problem_pg17.html

U.S. Department of Education. (2009). *Truancy: A serious problem for students, schools, and society*. Retrieved June 25, 2009 from http://www.ed.gov/admins/ lead/safety/training/truancy/index.html

U.S. Department of Education, Institute of Education Sciences (USDE IES). (2008). *IES practice guide: Dropout prevention*. Retrieved May 30, 2009 from http://ies.ed.gov/ncee/wwc/pdf/practiceguides/dp_pg_090308.pdf

U.S. Department of Justice Office of Juvenile Justice and Delinquency Prevention. (2007). *Tool kit for creating your own truancy reduction program*. Retrieved

August 27, 2009, from http://ojjdp.ncjrs.gov/publications/truancy_toolkit.
html

U.S. Government Accountability Office. (2005). *Report to congressional requesters: No Child Left Behind Act: Education could do more to help states better define graduation rates and improve knowledge about intervention strategies*. Retrieved May 27, 2009, from http://www.gao.gov/cgi-bin/getrpt?GAO-05-879

Walker, S., Spohn, C., & Delone, M. (2007). *The color of justice: Race, ethnicity and crime in America*. Belmont, CA: Thompson Wadsworth.

Wesley, T., & Duttweiler, P.C. (2005). Guidelines for evaluating truancy programs. National Dropout Prevention Center/Network. Clemson, SC: Clemson University.

What Works Clearinghouse (WWC). (2006a). Achievement for Latinos Through Academic Success. *Dropout Prevention*. U.S. Department of Education, Institute of Education Sciences. Retrieved November 30, 2009, from http://ies.ed.gov/ncee/wwc/reports/dropout/alas/index.asp What Works Clearinghouse (WWC). (2006b). *Dropout Prevention*. U.S. Department of Education, Institute of Education Sciences. Retrieved November 30, 2009, from, http://ies.ed.gov/ncee/wwc/reports/dropout/check_conn/.

What Works Clearinghouse (WWC). (2009). Coca-Cola Valued Youth Program. *Dropout Prevention*. U.S. Department of Education, Institute of Education Sciences. Retrieved November 30, 2009, from http://ies.ed.gov/ncee/wwc/pdf/wwc_ccvyp_052709.pdf.

White, M. D., Fyfe, J. J., Campbell, S. P., & Goldkamp, J. S. (2001). The school-police partnership: Identifying at-risk youth through a truant recovery program. *Evaluation Review, 25*(5), 507–532.

WhyTry. (2009). Retrieved June 15, 2009, from http://www.whytry.org

Wisconsin Legislative Audit Bureau. (2000). Truancy reduction efforts: A best practice review. *Journal of State Government, 73*(4), 13–16.

Zinth, K. (2005). *Truancy and habitual truancy*. Denver, CO Education Commission of the States. Retrieved February 3, 2009, from http://www.ecs.org/clearinghouse/61/16/6116.pdf

Index

Absence, 10
  and educational gap, 53
Academic slippage, 4
Academic tracking, 42–44
Achievement for Latinos Through
      Academic Success (ALAS), 83
Alcohol and drug use, 55–56
American Indians, truancy of, 36
Anger, and rage, 50
Assimilation, 44
Attendance, 4
  taxonomy, 5
Attendance Conciliation Team (ACT),
      of South Carolina Truancy Pilot
      study, 100, 101–2, 104
Attendance data
  collection of, 11–12
  and school social workers, 8
  tracking inconsistencies, 8
Attendance Improvement Mediation
      (AIM), in South Carolina
      Truancy Pilot study, 101
Attendance Intervention Plan (AIP), in
      South Carolina Truancy Pilot
      study, 99
Attendance Task Force, 5

BCSD. See Berkeley County School
      District (BCSD)
Behavior
  and attendance, 80–81
  in research-based programs,
      70, 75

Berkeley County School District
      (BCSD), 96, 98
Best practice, in truancy prevention/
      intervention. See Intensive
      individual interventions;
      School-wide interventions;
      Target group interventions
Blacks
  academic tracking of, 42, 43
  truancy of, 36, 37
Bush, George, W., 15

Check & Connect, 87–93
Coca-Cola Valued Youth Program,
      83–84
Community agencies collaboration,
      72–74
Conflict Solutions, 101–2
Crime, 55–58
  poverty and, 56

Disability, 30–36
  as behavior problem, 35–36
  case study, 30–35
Drop out, 52–54
  rate of, in United States, 5–7
Drug use. See Alcohol and drug use

Early Risers Skills for Success,
      82–83
Educational gap, 52–53
  and suspension, 51
  and teacher preparedness, 51

Educational outcomes, 53
Education Commission of the
    States, 17
Elementary school
    attendance data collection in, 11
Ethnic minority students
    and crime, 55
    truancy of, 50–51
Evidence, definition of, 62
Evidence-based practice, 8, 62, 75
    Websites, 63
Expulsion, 50–51

Familial relationship
    truancy and, 39
Family advocate, in Early Risers Skills
    for Success, 82
FBA. See Functional behavior
    assessment (FBA)
Federal and state legislation, 15–28
    recent policies, 15–16
Functional behavior assessment (FBA),
    80, 85
Funding
    lack of, 56–57. See also Poverty
    for research-based programs,
    67–68

Gay Lesbian Bisexual and
    Transgendered Competence
    Training, 38–40
Gay Lesbian Bisexual and
    Transgendered (GLBT)
    students
    truancy of, 38–40
Graduation rate, in United States, 5–7

High income schools, 52–53
High poverty schools, 47, 52
High school
    attendance data collection in, 11

Hinman, Pamela, 4–5
Hispanics, truancy of, 36

Impact, of truancy, 49–60
    on individual student, 52–56
    alcohol and drug use, 55–56
    crime, 55–56
    drop out, 53–54
    educational gap, 52–53
    educational outcomes, 53
    school discipline, 49–52
    on school system, 56–57
    on society, 57–58
Inferiority, feeling of, 38
Internet, as intervention programs
    resource, 62–63
Intensive individual interventions, Tier
    3, 85–93
    assessment at, 86
    mentoring, 86
    problem solving, parents and
    students in, 86–87
    research programs, 87–93
    support staff, role of, 87
In Touch (software), 100

Limbaugh, Rush, 44
Lions Quest, 76–77
Low-income schools, 52–53,
    56–57
Low-level academic tracking, 42
Low teacher expectation, 40–41, 43

Mediation, in truancy prevention, 101,
    102, 105
Microsoft Excel
    for attendance data collection, 12
Middle school
    attendance data collection in, 11
Monoculturalism, 44–45
Multiculturalism, 44–46

National Center for School
   Engagement (NCSE), 17
National Dropout Prevention Center
   (NDPC), 63
National Forum on Education
   Statistics, 5
National Registry of Evidenced-based
   Programs and Practices
   (NREPP), 62
NCLB. *See* No Child Left Behind Act
   (NCLB)
NCSE. *See* National Center for School
   Engagement (NCSE)
NDPC. *See* National Dropout
   Prevention Center (NDPC)
Negative stereotypes, 40–41
Neighborhood poverty
   and truancy, 47
No Child Left Behind Act (NCLB), 16
No Child Left Behind Law, 56
NREPP. *See* National Registry of
   Evidenced-based Programs and
   Practices (NREPP)

Office of Juvenile Justice and
   Delinquency Prevention
   (OJJDP), 63

Parental education, 47
Parental supervision, 48
Parents
   communication with, 72
   criminal prosecution for, 18
PBIS. *See* Positive Behavioral Intervention
   and Supports (PBIS)
Positive Behavioral Intervention and
   Supports (PBIS), 74–76
Poverty
   and crime, 56
   generational, 57
   and race, 47

Race, 36–38
   and multiculturalism, 45
   and poverty, 47
Reporting systems. *See* Tracking and
   reporting systems
Research-based program
   adaptations of, 66
   evaluation of, 66
   funding for, 67–68
   implementation of, 65–66
      checklist, 65
      fidelity of, 65
      readiness for, 64–65
Response to intervention (RtI), 61
"Responsive classroom" approach, 35
RtI. *See* Response to intervention (RtI)

SCDOE. *See* South Carolina
   Department of Education
   (SCDOE)
Schedule, and truancy, 72
Schlesinger, Arthur, 44
School climate, 46
School discipline, 49–52
   student–teacher relationship,
      51–52
School Refusal Assessment Scale for
   Children (SRAS-C), 86
School social workers, 13, 27–28,
   54, 59
   and attendance data, 8
   in South Carolina Truancy Pilot,
      95–109
   success story, 107–9
School-wide interventions, Tier 1,
   61–62, 69–72
   attendance recognition, 70–72
   communication with parents, 72
   community agencies, 72–74
   community-wide collaboration, 68
   funding, 67–68

School-wide interventions, Tier 1
(*Continued*)
goodness-of-fit in program
selection, 64–67
identification of, 62–63
research programs, 74–77
school climate improvisation,
68–69
student support staff, role of, 74
teachers and administrators'
attitude, 69–70
School-wide PBIS (SWPBIS), 74–76
Sexual orientation, 38–40
Single-parent students
academic tracking of, 42
Social school workers, 37–38, 40
Socioeconomic factors, and truancy,
46–48
South Carolina
code of laws in, 99
definition of truancy in, 99
South Carolina Department of
Education (SCDOE), 95–96
South Carolina Truancy Pilot, school
social workers in, 95–109
community agencies in, 101–2
funding for, 95–96
goal of, 96–97
lessons learned, 107
outcomes of, 105–6
district level, 106
school level, 106
partnership blueprint/MOA,
96–105
program planning/implementation,
98–105
assessment, 99
truancy levels, 99
attendance clerks in, 100
in student perspective, 105
in systems perspective, 105

SRAS-C. *See* School Refusal
Assessment Scale for Children
(SRAS-C)
Status offense, 17
Student support staff, 74
Suspension, 50–51
and educational gap, 51
SWPBIS. *See* School-wide PBIS
(SWPBIS)

Target group interventions, Tier 2,
80–85
multidisciplinary assessment,
80–81
problem solving, parents and
students in, 81
progress monitoring, 81
research programs, 82–85
support staff, role of,
81–82
Tracking and reporting systems,
3–13
elements of, 9–12
attendance and truancy data,
11–12
high-quality monitoring systems,
10–11
problems in, 8–9
Truancy. *See also individual entries*
definition of, 3
by U.S. states, 17–28
consequences for, 18–27
consequences of, 3–4
criteria difference of, 8–9
current estimates of, in United
States, 4–7
using graduation and dropout
rates, 5–7
family factors and, 46–48
socioeconomic factors,
46–48

impact of, 49–60
individual factors and,
    29–40
    disability, 31–36
    race, 36–38
    sexual orientation, 38–40
school factors and, 40–46
    academic tracking, 42–44
    multiculturalism, 44–46

school climate, 46
stereotypes and low expectation,
    40–41
role of school social workers, 27–28
Truancy Intervention Program, 33

WhyTry, 84–85
Working-class students
    academic tracking of, 42